Gerry Pye is a former RAF wing commander and chartered aeronautical engineer. After retiring from the RAF, he spent many years as an Open University associate lecturer specializing in engineering and global development management. He began writing on military history and aviation in 2000, and he became a full-time freelance writer in 2022 after a successful expedition to climb Mount Kilimanjaro. He lives in Cambridgeshire with his fiancée, Karen, and has a son, Joseph, who followed in his father's footsteps to pursue a career in aeronautical engineering.

To Lou

from Gerry x

*Reflections from the Top of the World* is for Andrew Fairlie and Wendy Marie Pye, who trekked with us in spirit from the very start to the very finish.

Gerry Pye

# REFLECTIONS FROM THE TOP OF THE WORLD

AUSTIN MACAULEY PUBLISHERS®

LONDON • CAMBRIDGE • NEW YORK • SHARJAH

A CIP catalogue record for this title is available from the British Library.

ISBN 9781035863549 (Paperback)
ISBN 9781035863556 (ePub e-book)

www.austinmacauley.com

First Published 2024
Austin Macauley Publishers Ltd®
1 Canada Square
Canary Wharf
London
E14 5AA

I would like to thank Karen James, Dr David Cochrane MBE, Jennie Cochrane, Mr Stuart Vincent BEM, and Joseph Pye, for their unfailing support and belief in me. I am also grateful to the people that encouraged me to 'just keep going', including my fellow Climbers on the Hospitality Industry Trust Scotland Kilimanjaro Expedition 2022, Tony and Alison Reeves for forming Band on the Run, the members of BRJ Run and Tri Huntingdon, and all the musicians that have helped me make the world a little better through mutual endeavour and achievement. I have learned a great deal from the writings and philosophies of others. All those I have referred to in the text have their relevant works listed in the bibliography at the end.

# Table of Contents

# The Climbers

Nico Baird
Alexandra Brennan
Stephen Brennan
David Cochrane MBE
Jennie Cochrane
Annabel Drysdale
Jim Fairlie MSP
Craig Haddow
Barry Laurie
Richard Mayne
Stephen McNally
Callum McNally
Karl Mitchell
Gillian O'Brien
Paul O'Brien
Amanda Pirie
Michael Prior
Gerry Pye
Jennifer Robertson
Sophia Schwer
Roderick Young
Toby Wand

# Foreword

## By Dr David Cochrane MBE

In life, everyone has a metaphorical mountain to climb. This is part and parcel of the cycle of life, and no one knows when their moment will come. The author of *Reflections from the Top of the World*, Gerry Pye, had an illustrious career in the RAF and had a wonderful family, supporting him at every step of the way. As his formal service was coming to a natural conclusion, he was looking forward to the next chapter with positive enthusiasm. In a twist of fate, this is when his wife, Wendy, was diagnosed with breast cancer and passed away far too early.

Gerry threw himself into a myriad of voluntary undertakings to keep busy and to keep himself focussed on positive activities. One of these challenging activities was to join a group of predominantly Scottish hospitality people, to climb the highest free-standing mountain in the world— Kilimanjaro. Living in the flattest part of the UK in the Cambridge Fens, this was a serious undertaking. This book outlines some of the physical challenges that he and the group had to overcome to reach the summit. It also gives an insight into the drivers and motivators that can inspire some people or potentially break others.

This book can be read solely as an insight into the mechanics of going on an 8-day expedition in Tanzania or, on a much deeper level, it can give hope, confidence and solace that life's mountains can be overcome and a positive path can be found from within a dark starting point.

Gerry was an excellent member of the 22-person expedition, and he has captured the momentous highs and the sometimes comical moments of each day spent circumnavigating the 'Roof of Africa'. This book will make you laugh, it will make you think about the fragility of life and relationships, and it will give you courage to face challenges head-on. It is not always about the journey of life; it's about the people you share that journey with.

# Introduction

Mount Kilimanjaro is a dormant volcano located in Kilimanjaro Region of Tanzania. It has three volcanic cones: Kibo, Mawenzi and Shira. It is the highest mountain in Africa and the highest single free-standing mountain above sea level in the world: 5,895 m above sea level and about 4,900 m above its plateau base. Climbing Mount Kilimanjaro is extremely demanding both physically and mentally, but despite its enormous height it can be successfully climbed with minimal technical skill. Even so, for every 3 climbers that set out, only 2 make it to the summit. The 2022 expedition to climb Mount Kilimanjaro was organised by the Hospitality Industry Trust (HIT), Scotland, and comprised 22 climbers; only one of whom had successfully climbed the mountain before. Given the poor success rate, would all 22 climbers make it to the top?

HIT Scotland is a unique charity that provides scholarships and placement opportunities for people wishing to learn and develop skills in a wide range of hospitality disciplines. I did not know too much about HIT Scotland's extraordinary work at the time, only that the purpose of the expedition was to raise funds to support a new scholarship it had created in memory of Andrew Fairlie who, sadly, died of a brain tumour in January 2019. Andrew was a world-renowned chef operating his double Michelin-starred restaurant at Gleneagles Hotel and Resort in Auchterarder, Perth and Kinross.

I had lost my wife, Wendy, in November 2018 after her long battle with cancer, and I was invited to join the Kilimanjaro expedition by HIT Scotland's chief executive, David Cochrane, who is married to Wendy's sister, Jennie. The expedition was originally due to take place in 2020, and I considered taking part an appropriate response to the heartbreak that cancer had caused our families. The Covid-19 pandemic delayed the trek by 2 years, and I almost did not join the postponed expedition in 2022—I thank providence that I did because climbing Mount Kilimanjaro changed my life in ways that I could not have possibly imagined.

Early in 2022, I set off on a trip around Europe that I had organised in 2019 shortly after losing Wendy. The trip had been put back owing to the pandemic and it comprised a rail journey on the Orient Express and a cruise around the Mediterranean Sea. These were things that Wendy had put on her bucket list but had not managed to complete before she died. I resolved to complete them for her, but the adventure proved to be one of the loneliest and most heartbreaking trips I had ever experienced. To cheer myself up, I read a self-help book that prescribed keeping a journal as part of a range of simple ideas to promote happiness. I discovered that keeping a journal of my experiences on the cruise did exactly that, I was able to reflect on how I felt about things and rationalise them in a different context.

Journaling became my saving grace. It was therefore a given that I was going to keep a journal to record my experiences, and indeed my feelings, when I embarked on the challenge to climb Mount Kilimanjaro. The following pages are transcribed from my expedition journal, which was written between 6 and 22 October 2022.

As my fellow climbers will no doubt recall, the temperature dropped very quickly on the mountain after the early evening sunset. Rather than be sat shivering around the camp tables in the mess tent after our evening meal, I retired to my tent and curled up in my sleeping bag to record the events of the day—I spent the next few hours merrily scribbling away under the light of my headtorch until settling down to sleep, with maybe the odd sortie into the cold night air now and again to relieve myself. There was no desk in the tent to rest against and no grammar or spell checker to correct the many mistakes I made as I scrawled wildly.

Originally, I had intended to transcribe the journal entries faithfully, but some of the mistakes were too egregious to leave uncorrected, and some of my jottings proved to be unintelligible even to me. Moreover, some of the feelings I transcribed were too deeply personal to be published more widely. Nevertheless, much of the prose and the broad context in which the words were written remains unchanged. The footnotes were added later for clarity.

I placed the journal on the shelf soon after returning from Africa, never intending to look at it again, at least not for a few years or so. The journal was quietly gathering dust until one day, Barry Laurie contacted me with a request for information. He was preparing a presentation and knowing that I had maintained a journal throughout the expedition, Barry asked me for details of what we had all been doing on a certain day. It turned out that Barry had been mentioned in

my journal on the day in question and I recorded a voicemail for him transcribing the events as I had witnessed them.

It had been a particularly brutal part of the climb, and I wrote that Barry had been talking to me about the local flora and fauna on the descent from the Barranco Wall, and I had commented that I was so exhausted that none of his words were registering. I ended the narrative saying that I hoped Barry did not think I was being rude. It then occurred to me that rather than sit on the shelf doomed to oblivion, the journal should be transcribed and given to the climbers as a lasting record of our adventure. This book is the outcome.

During my various incarnations as a student, I never appreciated the value of reflection. In my post-graduate studies, my lecturers impressed on me the need for balance in terms of research, analysis, and reflection. I understood research as an examination, finding facts, discovering the art of the possible. I had come to terms with analysis a being the means through which we attain understanding; however, I never gave much thought to reflection. I contextualised it as being the 'so what' at the end of an argument—what are the wider implications of the knowledge and insights gained from the research and analysis?

As an older and wiser lecturer, I came to appreciate the power of reflection; to put previous learning and/or understanding into the context of new experience and/or new technological developments—and vice versa; to continually review where the balance of argument lies in order to keep an open mind. Doing so cleverly achieves new insights into things that may have been taken for granted or overlooked, perhaps enabling you to see things—the world even—from a whole new perspective. Reflective practice is a means of continually learning from real-life experiences and works best as an analytical process that asks why instead of just being descriptive. Why did I feel the way I did, why did I behave the way I did, why did I fail, why was I successful?

I have, therefore, found it hugely insightful when reflecting on how I felt during the expedition especially compared with how I feel now. I have found it fascinating to consider, for example, that I would dearly love to return to Kilimanjaro one day and conquer its peak once more, when my journal clearly implies that hell would freeze over before I would consider doing such a thing again. I have therefore extended each chapter, the narrative for each day of the trek, to include a reflective piece about how I feel now and/or the insights the experience gave me that I could or have applied to my life going forward. I hope that any of my fellow climbers reading this book will perhaps do the same.

To put the Kilimanjaro expedition into context, I had been struggling to rebuild my life in any meaningful way since Wendy died. I had taken redundancy from my job as an associate lecturer for the Open University, thinking that I had no love for it; however, I missed the interaction with the students hugely. I missed the fulfilment lecturing delivered in terms of helping other people improve their lives. I had also quit the Royal Air Force Wyton Voluntary Band, thinking that I was not a sufficiently accomplished musician to do justice to the endeavour, but I missed playing music too. I missed the thrill of marching along Huntingdon High Street thumping my bass drum to the Royal Air Force March Past and playing my saxophone as part of a combined military-band at Peterborough Cathedral and many other prestigious venues.

Soon after Wendy died, I found myself having to deal with my elderly parents. I had to watch their lives fall apart as my father succumbed to Alzheimer's and Parkinson's disease with aphasia thrown into the mix, which meant my father could no longer speak. Owing to manifold issues throughout my childhood and through to my adult years, I had a difficult relationship with my father and was wrestling with the guilt of sparing my compassion for him as his health deteriorated. I was forcing myself to care for him for my mother's sake and it had become hugely detrimental to my mental wellbeing. I missed being with people and I was becoming a directionless, lonely old widower.

At the same time, I was having to deal with the pandemic and the mandated isolation. At the end of 2020, citizens were allowed to mingle again in England, and I was looking forward to spending time with family after being kept apart. In the run-up to the Christmas holidays in 2020, days and days of torrential rain caused the local brook to burst its banks. My house was flooded. Up to that point, I had not considered that the year 2020 could have become any worse, but Christmas Eve was spent tossing sodden carpets out the windows and turning the kitchen with its tiled floors into a temporary living room for the duration of the holidays and for the next 9 months as it turned out. The house was not restored until September 2021 with much upheaval suffered in the meantime. Subsequently, I have no peace of mind when it rains heavily, and I am still faced with a huge expense to protect the house from future flooding.

I had started a new relationship soon after losing my wife—too soon as it turned out—and this new association had fallen apart at the end of 2021. I can reflect on the breakup now and conclude that going our separate ways was the absolute best thing for both of us. It was nevertheless devastating and added further heartbreak to my already strained psyche. Unfortunately, seeing me with another lady in my life had not been easy for my family, especially my son Joe, who was only 17 years old when he lost his mother. He had done his best to control his feelings and after a while, he reached out to my 'girlfriend', whom he thought, selflessly on his part, would spare me from loneliness when he went off to university. He later embraced the idea of having a stepmother, and a stepbrother and stepsister, which would have made him no longer an only child.

Moreover, Joe accorded himself the title of 'uncle' when my girlfriend's daughter had a baby, and he was due to be best man at my wedding. Sadly, my relationship fell apart at a time when Joe truly began to grieve for his mother. I felt that I had let him down and I reproached myself for causing him yet more pain. Furthermore, my new relationship had served to estrange me from some of the people I loved and cared about most in the world—Wendy's family. I had never felt more alone.

Jennie and David Cochrane, Wendy's sister and brother-in-law, had been wonderfully supportive since Wendy died. Indeed, they had invited me to take part in the original Kilimanjaro expedition in 2020. Jennie and David showed me every kindness, but for reasons I am too ashamed to recount, I shunned their benevolence and withdrew from the expedition. My new relationship had rendered me myopic and unable to think rationally about the hurt I was causing, and the hurt being imposed on me; however, to my eternal joy and thankfulness, David reached out to me when my relationship collapsed. He had never formally struck me off the list of participants and reinstatement was a simple matter. So, come October 2022, I had a mountain to climb. I also had bridges to build.

My fellow climbers might also remember that things were not looking too good for the country in the autumn of 2022. The Russian invasion of Ukraine earlier in the year had shocked the world and created an energy crisis that tipped the fragile UK economy into crisis. The Queen and head of state for over 70 years had died and the country was coming to terms with a new King and Queen consort. At the same time, there were growing reports of pensioners not being able to afford to heat their homes, and everything seemed to be in a parlous state: the NHS, roads, rail networks, schools. There were migrant crises in the English Channel, and huge political instability at home and abroad.

Rampant inflation was causing a cost-of-living crisis the likes of which had not been seen since the 1970s. In the week before, we embarked on our trek, it was being reported in the media that the tax burden on UK citizens had increased to the highest level experienced since the Second World War, and yet there was no money for important public services such as social care, nor to address the 7,000,000 people languishing on NHS waiting lists. News bulletins had become an endless stream of doom and gloom—*nil desperandum*.

There was one bright spot in my life. Since the end of the summer, I had been dating Karen, a lovely lady from my running club. We were both taking things very slowly, but our relationship had been moving in the right direction. Karen had met Joe; not surprisingly, she had been very anxious about doing so, but he was charming and made Karen feel very welcomed at our family home. Joe was about to leave home permanently, and I suspect that he was beginning to fret a little about my being alone. Joe's approval was paramount and gladly received, but I was still reluctant to tell Jennie and David about Karen, given the family sensitivities. I had to make sure I approached the topic more carefully and sensitively, and it was Karen herself that coined the moto: 'A Mountain to Climb, Bridges to Build'.

Against this backdrop, I gathered my kit together to climb the largest free-standing mountain in the world.

# Thursday 6 October 2022

I set off from Wistow[1] at 0710 heading for Newport Pagnell service station on the M1[2]. I was excited and glad to have a break from my village. I was also thankful to be getting on with the trip as it has been on and off for the last 3 years, and it was important for me to properly reconnect with Jennie and David and put the turmoil of the last 3 years behind us in more ways than one.

I decided not to use the Mercedes Satnav after the trauma I experienced on my return from the gala dinner on the Royal Yacht Britannia on the day the Queen died—my Satnav seemed overly keen to send me down single-lane country roads with 400 miles of journey left to do. Happily, I met Toby Wand and his wife at Newport Pagnell service station as agreed, and they both seemed lovely. After a brief introduction, we set off on the long trip to Edinburgh, which according to Waze[3] was over 300 miles away. Initially, the

---

[1] Wistow, a small village near Huntingdon in Cambridgeshire.

[2] Toby Wand lives in England and although we had never met, we arranged to travel to Scotland together.

[3] Waze was the iPhone navigation app I was using in lieu of the Mercedes Satnav.

journey went well, and the weather was particularly kind to us while we were in England. Just north of the border, the heavens opened, and I had to slow right down, which meant that the arrival time started getting later as a result. Nevertheless, we arrived in Edinburgh in good time and waited in the hotel lounge for Jennie and David to pitch up.

When Jennie and David arrived, me and Toby had to repack our gear into the North Face duffle bag provided by one of the sponsors—Tiso and We are Extraordinary Training—and very resplendent these bags were too. Later we met some more of the trekkers and had burgers and chips in the hotel restaurant. Some of the Scottish women's football team were in the restaurant, and what a miserable bunch they were. I did not attempt to get pictures and/or autographs but devoured my food thinking that this would be the best scran I was likely to eat for the next 2 weeks. We also had a couple of cheeky pints laid on by the hotel, so not a bad start to the trip.

Toby and I shared a twin room in the hotel, and we set the alarm for 0215. I hardly slept at all and when we mustered for the taxi, a wedding reception was just wrapping up in the hotel. The best man asked who we were, and it was amusing watching him try to articulate *Kilimanjaro* in his drunken state. He donated £20 to our charities, which was rather kind, but we could not help wondering whether he would remember doing so once he had sobered up. The flight to Schiphol was quite pleasant; KLM is a top-drawer airline, and I was proud to note that my son, Joe, had just started working for it.

\*\*\*

people compared with the convivial setting of the hotel bar. I had no idea then just how important to me these people would become.

ne. Joe was about to leave home
at he was beginning to fret a little
 approval was paramount and
ill reluctant to tell Jennie and
 family sensitivities. I had to
 topic more carefully and
rself that coined the moto: 'A
Build'.

ered my kit together to climb
 in the world.

# Sunday 9 October 2022

So much has happened in the last few days that I haven't had time to put pen to paper. It was Karen's birthday yesterday and I was so lucky to be able to send her birthday wishes—I had full connectivity in the Ngorongoro Crater and could send and receive pictures and messages in real time. Unfortunately for Karen, she had contracted Covid—poor girl. Now here's the rub, I have seen so many amazing sights while I have been in Africa. I have experienced many different and exciting things but all the time I am thinking about Karen. That's a good thing in some respects, but I still do not want to fall head over heels for her because I really do not want to put my heart on the line again—but I don't seem to be able to help myself.

I am currently sat on the balcony of my lodge in Tanzania, and it is so peaceful. I say that a bit advisedly because I could not sleep through the almighty dawn chorus. I think it was only a couple of birds, but they did not half make a racket. Yesterday we were in Ngorongoro Crater—an old extinct volcano and natural sanctuary for African wildlife. It was nearly a 6-hour trip to get there in a battered jeep, but I managed to catch up with some sleep after the 0520 reveille. This was the first time that I was able to take in my environment and it did not take long for me to appreciate how lucky I was to live in the UK.

The poverty was breathtaking. The roads were lined with half-built shanty-style properties made from breeze blocks with no pavements or tarmacked roads beyond the main throughfares. There were shops of sort, and I observed many people sat on motorcycles, which our guide told us were actually taxies. Many of the people were shoddily dressed in dirty, western-style coats and trousers with flip-flops or trainers on their feet. Others seemed to be dressed in more traditional African attire—which comprises a brightly coloured blanket (Shuka) fashioned into a sort of dress, with a colourful headdress for the women. I saw several women walking along the road carrying bundles on their heads, all neatly balanced, and I was impressed with their poise and elegance.

The guide explained that the settlements were established along the main roadside because that gave them access to electricity and water. But the buildings were very austere to say the least. Every now and then an opulent church appeared that dominated the local town buildings. Then occasionally a grand mansion house came into view, which I suspected were probably the main house on a plantation. It was hard to imagine anything growing in the fields around these plantations, as the dirt was dry and full of rocks. Nevertheless, we did come across some lush fields and well laid out banana plants. The main local crop appeared to be coffee.

There were also some goat herds in amongst the townsfolk that appeared to be grazing on the grass between the roads and the settlements, although there did not appear to be much grass for them to eat. As we approached the main town, Arusha, the standard of the buildings gradually improved and the people started to appear better presented— very few overweight people, but some of the ladies were portly about the waist. We came across a group of runners, and it occurred to me that it was park run[4] day in UK and that my friends back home would be lining up at the local park to perform the Saturday morning ritual. The runners we passed were arranged in 3 ranks, with individuals holding flags front and back.

We eased passed them in our jeep and they were singing. It was a sort of chant and response song that matched the cadence of the run, but not like the USMC[5] chanting—this singing was very noticeably African, not unlike the Zulu chanting in the film of the same title. Our guide told us that they were police cadets out for an early morning run. I was quite taken by the spectacle.

As the journey progressed the traffic became denser and soon these 3-wheeled taxis, the tuk-tuks more commonly associated with Asian cities, began to dominate the traffic. The Tanzanians drive like absolute maniacs, overtaking on blind summits and driving onto the verges, but there appeared to be an unwritten rule that you let the driver overtaking slide in front of you if traffic is approaching from the opposite direction. There was lots of honking as the buses and cars overtook. In the city, more and more people appeared in western-style attire and there were recognisable brands such as Vodafone appearing in the roadside shops, and I saw

---

[4] Park run is a free to enter timed run over 5km that happens nationally and globally on Saturday mornings.

[5] United States Marine Corps.

several big brand car showrooms—Toyota seemed to be the most prevalent. One of the most striking things I saw was a security guard outside a bank armed with an AK47[6] assault rifle.

I should mention that we lost one member of our party back in Edinburgh—Craig Haddow did not have over 6 months remaining on his passport. He re-joins us today, but sadly he missed out on the safari. In the UK, we associate the word *safari* with purposely trekking across Africa to see the unique wildlife; however, I learned that safari is a Swahili word that means *travel*. So, we were on safari (travelling) to Ngorongoro Crater to see the wildlife. We left the town of Arusha behind us and for a few hours, the road was smooth and the scenery featureless. Every now and then, we saw Massai dressed in their bright-coloured shukas, leading goats with their double pointed spears—some of which were no more than wooden sticks. Some of the goat-herders looked very young—mostly boys. Every now and then, a traditional Massai settlement appeared—mud huts as we would call them in the UK. They seemed very sturdy.

I drifted off to sleep on the smooth roads, which was easier than you would imagine having been up before dawn twice in a row after a long journey from the UK.

Presently, we turned off the main road onto an orange-coloured dirt track that kicked up clouds of thick dust. We often lost sight of the jeep in front of us in the dust clouds and

---

[6] AK-47, *Avtomat Kalashnikova*, a gas-operated assault rifle developed in the Soviet Union by Mikhail Kalashnikov in 1947, which—according to Jane's Defence Weekly—is the most prolific firearm in the world.

the journey took on a sort of *Top Gear* feel—it was very bumpy and dusty, and we were also climbing. I knew this was the case because every now and again the cliff edge appeared between the trees and in most cases, it was a sheer drop.

We arrived at the grand entrance to the park and were shown a model of the crater, which as I have already mentioned was the site of an old volcano. This had blown up Mount St Helena's style many millennia ago[7]. The model showed that we were just to the south of the Serengeti Plain, but the model did not do the crater justice. We trekked on in the jeeps along the orange dusty tracks until we came to a viewpoint. It was pretty much the same location from which I had viewed the model, but it could not have been more of a contrast.

I do not have the words to explain how beautiful it is. The spectacle was reminiscent of a scene from the Disney film, *Lion King*. Our convoy descended into the crater and passed dozens of the flat-topped trees[8] I had only ever seen before on television or characterised in the *Jungle Book*. I had no idea looking from the top of the escarpment just how teaming the crater was with wildlife. We first saw a small herd of wildebeest and zebras, and the guide explained that these

---

[7] I learned subsequently that the Ngorongoro Crater was a *caldera* which forms when the mountain top sinks into the void left behind when the magma has all erupted—so not a Mount St Helen's event as I had tried to understand the formation at the time.

[8] These trees are called *Vachellia tortilis*, and they arch dramatically over the savannah with their distinctive flat tops throughout Ngorongoro Crater.

creatures often herded together to increase their numbers and their safety.

*The Ngorongoro Crater: the world's largest inactive volcanic caldera and a stunning game reserve southeast of the Serengeti in northeastern Tanzania.*

\*\*\*

The poverty I witnessed was very striking, and depressing. I had studied and taught global development management for nearly 15 years and could not help wondering about why the international community was not making a difference here in Tanzania. What was holding them back? Why were people still living in squalor, in substandard shelters with no tarmacked roads in their villages? Tanzania undoubtedly has an army, a well-trained police force, hospitals, dispensaries, and children were clearly being educated, which is indicative of a functional civic society that raises taxes and provides public services.

Are there structural issues surrounding the distribution of wealth? Poor leadership, exploitation, corruption, civil war? It was not easy to gather evidence looking out of the window of my jeep as we passed through these communities, but it struck me as odd that after decades of international intervention in Africa, poverty was still rife.

Most people my age learned about Africa in geography lessons under the label of a third-world country. Happily, we now use the less pejorative and patronising term 'developing nation'[9], but development appears on the face of it to be woefully slow. As children in the 1970s we were exposed to the huge famines in Africa, particularly Ethiopia where television news was replete with images of *human skeletons* suckling pot-bellied babies—starvation on a biblical scale. We saved tin foil, milk bottle tops, old clothes, and paperback books, and watched the Blue Peter 'Totalizer' light up each week as the appeal target was reached. Thankfully, I did not see any evidence of starvation during my time in Africa, but why had decades of development activity made little difference to most of the Tanzanian population. It is a complex issue with no simple answers.

Reflecting on my trip to Africa has been hugely insightful, mostly in terms of how my thinking developed as the adventure unfolded. As I pore though the scribbled writing, I

---

[9] The term 'developing nations' is becoming less relevant as it assumes a hierarchy among countries. The World Bank no longer singles out developing nations but instead focuses on sustainable development goals for the whole world.

can see now that I gained so much more from the expedition than I could ever have hoped for. Indeed, at the start of this adventure, I clearly had no cognizance of where the journey would lead. I set out hoping to conquer a mountain and to reconnect with my late wife's family, but I ended up with a richer philosophy for living a meaningful life. In the years since Wendy died, I convinced myself that it would be difficult to live my life without love, in all its forms; yet here I am being cynical about love in the opening paragraph of my journal entry for Sunday 9 October 2022.

My secondary education took place at Heronswood School in Welwyn Garden City, Hertfordshire. The school has long since been demolished and replaced with a housing estate, and yet there remains a willow tree in the middle of the estate that serves as a place of pilgrimage. This tree was in the middle of the school quadrangle, and it is the only part of the school that survived the redevelopment. I have visited this tree several times to reflect on my school days and one detail that always springs to mind is the poem *Desiderata* by Max Ehrmann. My headmaster used to read this poem in the final assembly before the end of every school term—and I can say with conviction that I never listened to it. Indeed, the opening line of the poem: *Go placidly amid the noise and the haste...* was invariably greeted with a mournful groan from the student cohort eager to start the holiday.

*Desiderata* has since become one of my favourite poems. It literally means *something desired* and Max Ehrman effectively provides a route map to navigate the trials of life with a final entreaty: *strive to be happy*. Ehrman invites us to be ourselves and to not feign affection. *Neither be cynical about love; for in the face of all aridity and disenchantment, it is as perennial as the grass.* That meant nothing to me in my teenage years, but when I reflected on my life from the top of the world, I realised that this is true, love is perennial—nevertheless, it is not always easy to find, it must be nourished and cherished, and it can also be fleeting, and it is not without risk.

An extraordinary occurrence happened while I was writing this reflective piece on *Desiderata.* A post appeared on a former Heronswood School pupil's Facebook page, that I had forgotten all about, saying that our former headmaster, Graham Thorp Kingsley, had died on 13 August 2023. Hundreds of his former pupils offered their condolences to Mr Kingsley's family, and nearly all of them recounted his reading *Desiderata* at the end of term.

I was astonished to read the testimonies of so many former pupils, even the erstwhile school bullies and troublemakers, eulogising about how much the poem now meant to them, even though, like me, they had groaned at the opening line and did not listen attentively. Mr Kingsley carried on as if the groan had not occurred, he never paused or stumbled, and just soldiered on until the piece was delivered and the holidays commenced. Such was the genius of the man, that he somehow knew that we were listening, and that we would all eventually appreciate *Desiderata*, and understand why he impressed the messages therein upon us. He knew that one day we would reflect on those words and be better citizens for doing do. As a tribute to Mr Kingsley, I have transcribed the full original text as part of the epilogue. Rest in peace, Headmaster, you were truly a remarkable man.

# Monday 10 October 2022

Narrating how many and which species I saw in the park would be too difficult, there were so many. I was thrilled to see the Thompson gazelles and the wildebeest, and I managed to get some decent photographs of most of them; however, we struggled to get close enough to the elephants to get a good picture and the lions we saw were sleeping in a gully, beautifully camouflaged.

After a brilliant morning, we pulled up for lunch by the lake, which we soon discovered was full of hippopotamuses (hippos). The guides explained that there were no crocodiles in the park owing to the natural barrier of the crater rim. So, we stood by the lake quite safely—or so we thought—and watched the hippos bobbing up and down in the water, snorting loudly and flicking their ears each time they surfaced. They were very close by, and Amanda merrily reported that hippos were responsible for more human deaths than any other animal in Africa. I quipped: "What are we doing standing here for then!"

On the way out of the park, we passed a small rest room at a ranger station and Barry, one of our travelling companions, asked if the jeep could be reversed so he could 'ease springs'[10]. We all sighed, but when we were reversing along the track, we saw a massive bull elephant complete with huge tusks, minding his own business in the woods. It was the money shot of the trip so far. Thank goodness for Barry's bladder.

We travelled back to the lodge—a different one from where we started—and we had a dip in the pool. It was bracing to say the least. Nevertheless, it was very refreshing, and the gin and tonics dished out at the poolside bar were a welcome bonus. Dinner was exceptional; stir fry and barbeque chicken, and you were able to choose the stir fry ingredients yourself, which were cooked in front of you in frighteningly hot woks. Later during the meal, the staff paraded through the mess hall singing a traditional Swahili song, *Hakuna Matata*, which created a good atmosphere. I had a couple of bottles of the local brew and then turned in.

On Sunday, we headed back to Ngorongoro to climb our first mountain and I was particularly nervous about doing so given my lack of training—I need not have worried. We set off with one man down, Paul O'Brien; he had pulled a muscle in his back the day before and decided to give himself another day to recover. The trip to the mountain was around the crater

---

[10] '*Ease springs*' is a term used in military firearms training. The range marshal calls for the working parts of the weapons to be held back and locked against the springs so that he/she can inspect the chamber to ensure that the weapon is unloaded. Once satisfied, the range marshal calls: '*Clear! Ease Springs!*' whereupon the working parts of the weapon are allowed to spring forward to close the chamber and thus the tension is removed from the springs. The terms '*ease springs*' is also military banter for relieving one's bladder.

rim to the other side of the Ngorongoro Plain and we stopped halfway to pick up our lion guard. His name was Hilari, a park ranger, and he boarded one of our jeeps clutching his AK47 with a folding stock. He turned out to be a very charming young man and he spoke marvellous English, something he was very proud of. He explained that in the event of a lion prowling us, he would shoot into the air to scare it off. Very comforting considering that there were no fences between us and where we had seen the lions the day before.

*The Author with Hilari, who joined us on the acclimatization climb to the west of the Ngorongoro crater to scare off any lions encountered along the way.*

The road trip on the other side of the park took us through some Massai villages, or bomas, and the children waved to us as we passed. We stopped at a boma to start our climb and one of the villagers joined our party to guide us on the mountain. The boma elder was resplendent in his traditional red shuka, but he was wearing grey ankle socks and tartan slippers, which spoiled the effect somewhat. He was very clean and well presented, which was more than could be said for the children. They were all dressed in dirty clothes, some of which looked like western-style hoodies with English slogans written on them. I considered that when you put your old clothes in the charity bag that this village in Africa was typical of the places that the old clothes would end up. Some of the larger children wore shukas and carried the double-tipped Massai spears as they herded their goats and cows. This seemed to be the main occupation.

All the Massai settlements comprised an array of mud huts, with several stockades to protect the animals at night. I had thought that the stockades were called bomas, but this is the collective term for the huts and stockades combined. The stockades themselves were quite impressive and comprised tightly packed wooden vertical staves formed into a circle. The herder's job was to take the animals to pasture during the day and then herd them to the safety of the stockade in the evening—7 days a week. Today was Sunday and we saw some relatively well-dressed Massai going to chapel. There was also a school that served the district close by the boma, that was ringed with a barbed wire fence—supposedly to keep the lions out rather than to keep the children in. One special moment occurred when David Cochrane gave one of the Massai children a packet of Walker's biscuits, which contained two fingers of shortbread. The child broke the two shortbread fingers into pieces and shared them between what I presumed were his siblings. He did not hesitate and had no intention of keeping the food all for himself. It was rather touching to see.

*Two young Massai children sharing two fingers of Walker's shortbread.*

The trek to the top of the mountain would take us through several other Massai villages and most of the Massai just stood and looked at us as we passed through. We always called *Jambo* to say hello and waved at them. Some waved back and smiled, and they all had pearly white teeth. I did see some disturbing sights: small children, probably as young as

7 or 8 years old were wearing bundles that contained a swaddled baby. The guide explained that even though the girls were too young to herd cows or goats, they could help the community by looking after the babies. I could not help but respect these hardy people and I reflected on all the moaning back in the UK about the so-called cost-of-living crisis and the fall in living standards. Even the poorest people in the UK do not suffer the hardships that the Massai endure as part of their everyday lives.

*A young Massai tending his goats close to his boma.*

We progressed up the mountain and initially I found the going extremely hard work. My leg muscles complained, and I could feel my heart pounding. My breathing was hard, and I was feeling the effects of the altitude. I quickly found my rhythm, that said, and soon into the climb I felt very energetic and fit. There would be many moments of breathlessness, particularly on the steeper slopes, but I knew that I was fit enough to do the challenge. The same could not be said for everyone.

The first drama was when the right heel on Toby's boot started to come adrift from the sole. He asked if anyone had any gaffer tape, and I duly produced some tape from my pack and carried out some battle-damage repairs. Then Barry could not open his ration pack and so I produced my Leatherman multi-tool and cut a hole in the wrapping; I neglected to put the tool away properly. Halfway into the climb, Sophia succumbed to stomach cramps, and I stopped to help her. I offered her some of my water, which contained electrolyte, and then accompanied her for a few hundred metres before she cramped up again. One of the guides had to take her back to the jeeps; unfortunately, when I took my pack off to help Sophia, I dropped the Leatherman—it was lost forever after owning said multi-tool for over 25 years. At first, I was mightily upset; however, I soon became a bit more philosophical about it. I told myself that a Massai herder would find it and would either put it to good use or trade it for something his family could use.

So now, we were two climbers down. The slopes appeared to become steeper and steeper as we approached the summit and Alexandra (Lexie) began to fall behind. She bravely tried to continue, and I did my best to support her; I even offered to carry her pack. She rallied for a while, and I left her with 2 of the guides that assured me they would stay with her. By the time I decided to move on, the rest of the party were over 200m further up the hill. I made haste to catch up with them and then looked down to see that Lexie was still struggling. I then found myself alone and thought it was a good time to fetch out the harmonica. I looked over the valley at the scenes reminiscent of a scene from the film, *Out of Africa*[11], and I played the Last Post. It was a very special moment. As I caught up with my companions, the main guide was leading them in a singsong. There is something quintessentially African about the working song—it was amazing. Soon after, we reached the top and duly claimed our first peak.

*Older Massai goatherds would guide their goats and cattle to the lush pasture in the hills above the Boma, remaining vigilant for predators at all times.*

On the way back, I fell nicely into a supporting role and helped the rear party negotiate the rocks and I generally kept an eye on them. We eventually made it back to the jeeps where the casualties were waiting for us and, understandably, they were eager to get back to the lodge. The drivers duly

---

[11] '*Out of Africa*', 1985, an epic romantic drama starring Meryl Streep and Robert Redford.

obliged, and it was very much a white-knuckle ride home. So ended our first climb in Africa. I had a dip in the pool and a gin and tonic, and after dinner I went back to my lodgings to bed.

David Cochrane, or Big D as I called him, told everyone that we had to be loaded on the transport and ready to go at 8am (0800). I was at the jeeps at 0750 in true military fashion with bags all packed and ready to go. I saw a fellow trekker and asked where everyone was. "They're still in breakfast!" came the reply. We did not get the jeeps loaded until 0830 and I found it quite infuriating, but I was learning not to *sweat the small stuff*, as Olivia Newton John said before she lost her battle with cancer. I think that Big D understood the climbers better than I did and stipulated an 0800-start knowing that it would be nearer to 0830—the warrant officer's half-hour as we called it in the service.

*A docile male elephant spotted grazing in the Ngorongoro Crater.*

*Getting up close and personal with one the Ngorongoro's tallest inhabitants – a Giraffe.*

\*\*\*

I reflect on the austerity and hardship associated with the Massai Bomas constantly. I implied in my journal that people in the UK did not know poverty compared with the poverty experienced in Africa—especially in those Massai villages we passed through during our first training climb. Poverty is a complex issue and making objective comparisons is far from being straightforward. The Massai might not consider themselves living in poverty, they are simply following a traditional, unchanging lifestyle. Their needs are very different to the UK citizens that find themselves suddenly unemployed, for example, with bills to pay, and food and clothing to buy on meagre benefits from the government.

People in the UK live in a consumerist society where essentials such as water and electricity need to be paid for. Where the Massai might forage wood from the jungle to lay fires for cooking, a UK citizen must procure a cooker and pay for the energy the cooker consumes—it is not sensible or helpful to suggest that those living in poverty in the UK should think themselves lucky because they do not have to live in a Massai boma.

Since returning from Africa, the cost-of-living crisis in the UK has become more acute. More and more citizens, even those in full employment, are relying on food banks and charity shops. It was churlish of me to ever consider that these UK citizens should think themselves lucky. I am very thankful to live in the UK but based on my experience passing through the Massai boma, I have decided that I have too many possessions. Just as I felt sure a Massai herdsman would benefit from finding my lost multi-tool, I am resolved to reduce my domestic inventory and pass on things I could certainly live without to make someone else's life a bit easier. How many citizens of the UK are hoarding possessions that they no longer use that could be put to good use elsewhere; indeed, should these hoarded belongings have even been acquired in the first place? We must collectively be sitting on millions of tonnes of mass-produced plastic and electronic components that are being stripped from the earth as natural minerals and eventually returned to the earth as landfill.

I often think about the simple kindness of the Massai child that shared the shortbread fingers with his companions. I observed a small community living in the most austere of settings, all depending on each other with even the smallest children contributing through herding goats or looking after babies. In a world of very few possessions, the simple kindness of sharing whatever was available to share appeared to create a bond of solidarity between the Massai children, a strong connection. Without necessarily thinking about it, I followed the children's example on the climb; whenever I found myself enjoying a rest break with a group of guides and porters, I would share my rations with them.

Passing around a handful of broken biscuits was a small but very well-received gesture that made me feel part of their group, even if it was only for a moment in time. As the expedition progressed, sharing items amongst our group increased. We swapped rations, shared cleaning products, lip salve, flavoured water—a veritable nightmare scenario had we been in lockdown during the recent pandemic. But this sharing proved to be highly conducive to our bonding as a group. The main observation that strikes me now many months after the event is that there was no expectations or obligations. None of us thought that because we shared our rations around the group that any debt was incurred or expectations of reciprocation—we shared for the pleasure of being part of a group, we shared for altruism. There were a few hiccoughs on the way, that said.

At dinner in the lodge the night before we returned to the Ngorongoro Crater to complete our first climb, I was still feeling awkward around my fellow climbers. I was still very much unconnected to them, and the conversations were rooted in familiar topics such as UK politics, the cost-of-living crisis, and the rights and wrongs of Lizz Truss's growth, growth, growth mantra. I had a heated discussion with Barry about the unfairness of the chancellor's taxation policies, in particular his cutting of the dividend allowance. I was bemoaning the fact that I had already paid corporation tax on the money lodged in my business account, and that should I have the temerity to withdraw funds from this account I would have to pay the chancellor a significant percentage for the privilege.

Barry, as a professional accountant, pointed out a few salient truths to me, which were not well received. Indeed, I took umbrage at his suggestion that in the eyes of the Inland Revenue, my limited company was not my personal property. I offered my opinion about the years of toil required to build a business and the huge risks involved. I also bemoaned the many years of careful financial planning undertaken to ensure that I would be comfortable in my retirement, all destroyed for a political expedient. Given the context in which we were having this debate, the issue was very much a 'first-world problem'. A surfeit of the local Kilimanjaro brew had undoubtedly raised our ardour.

In Desiderata, Ehrmann urges us to: *Speak your truth quietly and clearly; and listen to others, even to the dull and the ignorant; they too have their story.* I concede now in hindsight that I was the one being dull and ignorant, and Barry was listening to me. Happily, Barry and I quickly put the friction behind us the next day. I had very many interesting and thoughtful conversations with him on the mountain, and we shared several stories from our different life experiences. Happily, there was no alcohol on the trek.

# Day 1: Tuesday 11 October 2022

Yesterday, we endured another 'African massage' in the jeeps to go to Lake Manyara, which was about 160km due west of Kilimanjaro. We had hoped to see tree lions and flamingos, but as it turned out we saw neither. The lake had receded too much, so the flamingos had moved off somewhere else and as for the tree lions; they are camouflaged for a reason. We drove slowly through the jungle with our heads poked out the rooves of the jeeps looking for signs of these elusive creatures. It was amazing to see the leopard-type spots on the tree branches, which were caused by the sun's rays shining through the tree canopy. I had often wondered why the big African cats were spotted—brilliant camouflage in such a setting. Incidentally, today (10 October 2022) was the first day that it had been properly sunny and there were no clouds in the sky.

We did, however, see plenty of monkeys and baboons, along with a vulture with babies in a nest high in the trees. We also saw several hornbills, *hondo-hondo* as the locals call them. When we arrived at the lake edge, we saw herds of baboons of all shapes and sizes (not sure if herd[12] is the right

---

[12] According to English Grammar, a group of Baboons is called a Troop.

term). Some had tiny baboons clinging to their bellies and others were walking along with slightly bigger baby baboons perched on their backs—again it was generally peaceful. After another drive through the jungle, we saw a small male elephant and a hippo, and many more baboons.

We arrived at the picnic area on the hill overlooking the lake. There were some tables and chairs under a canopy of trees, and we had the most extraordinary view. During lunch, we were visited by several colourful birds, and one shat on my shoulder—yes, I did mean 'shat'. Allegedly, this is supposed to be good luck.

During lunch, we suddenly heard high-pitched screaming, which we assumed was coming from the baboons. In a clearing below us at the bottom of the hill, we saw many baboons running and initially I thought they were being chased by a lion, but it turned out to be an antelope.

*Note to self, the next time we come on safari remember to bring some binoculars.*

It turned out to be a whole herd of antelopes, which had obviously been spooked by something. So, for a few minutes we were treated to baboons and antelopes running through the clearing in the jungle below us.

After lunch, we came straight back to Arusha passing through the shanty towns as we journeyed east. We were travelling about the same time as the school day was finishing. The roads were lined with children of all shapes and sizes walking home in their school uniforms. I had been wondering how the Massai made money or bartered their goats and cattle. The jeep drove past several markets where the tribesmen were clearly selling/bartering their goats and alongside there were stalls selling shoes and clothes, hardware, etc. The verges and gullies along the roads and in the settlements were covered in litter—mostly plastic bottles.

We all became a bit nervous as we approached the new lodge because the jeep had to turn off the metalled road onto a dirt track, which was in an even worse state than the tracks in the park. There were men digging ditches by hand. There was also a huge digger that was moving mud ahead of our bus and the road was no more than a pile of orange mud with two flattened tracks in the middle where vehicles had driven previously. There was a small yellow people carrier in front of us labelled 'School Bus', and it was full of small school children.

Further down the track, the bus stopped, and a couple of them debussed. They could not have been more than 6 or 7 years old. They wore dusty school uniforms complete with ties and jumpers, and the smallest of them was wearing a beanie hat, which was clearly issued as part of his uniform. They disappeared into the jungle and waved to us as they did so. I would never have let Joe walk home from the bus stop at Wistow[13] on his own at that age, never mind walking home through the African jungle.

Our transport eventually arrived safely at the lodge, and we said our goodbyes to the drivers and guides. With a final song and a final issue of tips, we said our farewells. It was quite emotional. After a bottle of beer, we met our chief guide for the Kilimanjaro climb for the first time. His name was

---

[13] Wistow is the small village in Cambridgeshire just north of Huntingdon where I live.

John, but we were invited to call him Tony Blair because he had once climbed Kilimanjaro wearing a hoodie that had 'Tony Blair Foundation' emblazoned on the back. So, everyone calls him Tony Blair. My initial thought was that it was a good job he had not worked for Margaret Thatcher. Tony Blair told us that the locals referred to Mount Kilimanjaro as *Her Majesty*.

Briefing done, I went for a swim in the pool and then headed to the lodge to get ready for dinner. It was served on the lawn outside the main lodge under the stars and lit by candles. It was a barbeque buffet and I enjoyed it very much. Afterwards I sat around a huge firepit with my fellow trekkers, and we were filmed in turn explaining how we all felt on the eve of our epic climb. I simply explained that I was feeling good about the climb but was slightly nervous about meeting the challenge *Her Majesty* would present to a softy Englishman that lived in the Cambridgeshire fens.

Finally, the morning of the climb arrived. I was up, packed, fed, and abluted by 0730 and had time to write this journal. My roommate, Karl Mitchell, had not even packed his kit and I was thinking that everyone should do a bit of time in the armed forces. But again, Big D had called it right and had kept a bit in reserve. The next journal entry will be reporting my first experience of the mountain.

*Addendum*. I had a bit longer to wait for Karl, my roomy, so I thought I would just make a note of an extraordinary thing I saw on the acclimatisation climb 2 days ago. It appears that the Massai are beekeepers and they use wooden hives that they suspend from tree branches. These hives have a trapezium cross-section, and I am guessing they let the bees make their own honeycomb. I could not imagine that they would have the equipment that we use in the UK to examine the hives, or the means to control diseases and parasites such as the varroa mite[14]. Maybe they do not have varroa mites in Africa, and I am also guessing that they just eat the honey in their community and do not worry about separating brood from supers[15]. I would like to find out more.

*The next entry will be from 'Her Majesty', Mount Kilimanjaro.*

Well, here we are at Shira 1, the first camp on Kilimanjaro. I have just claimed my sleeping quarters and met my personal porter. His name is Richard, probably an assumed anglicised name to spare me the trouble of trying to pronounce his Swahili name. It is much colder than I was expecting, but totally bearable and I seem to be coping with the pace and altitude so far. I am sharing a tent with Karl, my roomy in the lodges, and we already know each other well after several nights together. He is as fit as a butcher's dog, and so he should be—he has completed several 'Ironman'[16]

---

[14] The Varroa mite is the bane of the UK beekeepers' lives. It is a tiny parasite that feeds off the adult bee and causes wing damage, which stops the bee from foraging. If left unchecked, the Varroa mite can wipe out a colony.

[15] In UK beekeeping, we split the hive into a brood box and what we call 'honey supers'. A grill or queen excluder is placed between the brood box and the supers so that the queen cannot enter the supers to lay her eggs, but the worker bees can still enter to deposit their honey. This makes it easier to harvest the honey.

[16] The Ironman® is a triathlon style race organized by the World

challenges, and he has a morning routine of sit-ups, press-ups and stretching.

We mustered at 0830 this morning, having dropped off our basecamp bags at the lodge reception. We met our driver 'Emanuel' and then we set off on the 4-hour trip to the ranger station at the bottom of the mountain, the start of the trail. We stopped off at a petrol station in Moshi to pick up some last-minute supplies and it was nice to stop and get in amongst the people. They are very different from the people that we met in the Massai Bomas. We had to fend off several street sellers, but eventually I succumbed and bought myself a wristband— it says *Hakuna Matata* in the Tanzanian colours of yellow, green and black. Hakuna Matata apparently means 'there are no problems'—no worries if you will.

Thankfully, the trek from the ranger station was tame. Not too much in terms of gradient and the pace was very steady. We were only on the trail for about 2 hours, no doubt the guides were breaking us in gently, and when our party arrived at the camp, we discovered that the porters had beaten us to it. I claimed my tent and my kitbag was already inside. I unpacked my sleeping kit and then it was time to scrounge a cup of tea before dinner, which was briefed for 1830.

The Climbers, as we now truly were, assembled outside the mess tent at the prescribed hour and had some tea. After tea, the porters sang us a traditional African song with a chant

---

Triathlon Corporation. The full event consists of a 2.4-mile swim, a 112-mile bike ride, and a 26.2-mile run; all to be completed in a time limit of 17 hours with cut-off times for each leg. Participants who finish within the time parameters achieve the prestigious title of 'Ironman'.

and counter chant, which I enjoyed very much. Then each of the porters (there were about 40 of them) introduced him or herself and even though most of them had English-sounding names, I knew I had no chance of remembering them all.

We then had to introduce ourselves saying in Swahili: "my name is …" I was one of the last to go and had ample opportunity to learn the phrase: *Jina langu ni Gerry!* I articulated the phrase as proficiently as I could, but probably mucked it up. It was hard to tell as the porters were unfailingly polite. That proved to be fun and then we went to the mess tent for dinner. A 3-course meal no less. Soup and bread, followed by fish in batter, spinach, roast potatoes, and a vegetable sauce a bit like a warm salsa. To finish, the chefs served fruit salad and more tea. This was my first experience of the nightly ritual of passing creamer, butter, thermos flasks and other accoutrements up and down the mess table. The chefs entered the tent after dinner, and they were applauded loudly.

It was then time for bed at about 2030, but there was not much else to do, and the temperature was dropping considerably; indeed, it was so cold that frost had started to form on the outside of the tent. Ironic that the first frost of the year I had witnessed was in Africa. I went to the lavatory tent, which Tony Blair had referred to as the *internet café*, to ease springs before turning in. After zipping the internet café doors shut, I walked back to the camp and when I was out in the middle of nowhere, I turned my head torch off. The stars were amazing. Of course, being in the southern hemisphere the constellations were all different and with no light pollution, the stars were especially bright. There was a full moon (or very nearly a full moon), and it was like daylight as I looked across the camp.

*The rudimentary mess tent where food and accoutrements were passed up and down the table every night after sundown.*

So, how do I feel after the first day on the mountain? I had a dream last night and it featured someone that had the form of my former girlfriend. She appeared totally differently in the dream, but to my subconscious mind, it was obviously her and I knew all the while I was under notice for her to leave me. We did various activities in the dream, but I was just wanting her to go so I could start the healing process. I think it might have been a metaphor for something I was experiencing—the workings of the human mind are ever perplexing. It was probably a side-effect of altitude sickness.

I generally do not think about my former girlfriend at all. Of course, I am faced with many wonders here in Africa and I should be distracted; however, every idle moment seems to be filled with thoughts about Karen. I have been wary of falling in love with her, but I know that I must already love her as I am missing her! Up to now, I have been able to message her and some of her replies have been lovely and heart-warming—she is such a sweetheart! Someone I am very much looking forward to seeing again when I arrive home.

I have also enjoyed getting to know my fellow trekkers and telling them about my experiences in the Royal Air Force. I have also enjoyed prattling on about my second career as an Open University Lecturer. I know in my heart that I have so much more to give and that this trip should be a reset for me. I think I can continue to contribute through my writing, and I must 'clear the pitch' when I return home to ensure that there are no further delays to relaunching this career. The time between the end of this trip and the New Year should be spent completing all the outstanding work services and making sure that plans for the flood defences are generated, approved, funded, and put out to tender[17].

I also need to re-attack the Ouse Valley Way Marathon[18] and make sure that I own it and take all reasonable steps to make it a stunning success. So much to look forward to.

---

[17] Work Service is the term I use for a household job such as painting the skirting boards, and one of the big jobs I must do is protect the house from future flooding.

[18] The Ouse Valley Way Marathon is a trail run along the River Great Ouse in Cambridgeshire, which my running club organises every year. I must have been having a stretch when they called for a volunteer race director and seeing my hand raised stitched me for the job—not true obviously.

Indeed, to reflect Charles Handy's[19] route to happiness, i.e., something to do, someone to love and something to look forward to—I'm doing all right.

***

When I was transcribing my journal into print, I soon realised that when I was on the mountain I appeared to be writing so much more. This was no doubt a result of how much time I had on my hands. It was too cold to loiter in the mess tent after dark, but some brave souls from the party congregated to play card games or to watch videos on their smartphones. I wanted to write, and this was best carried out in the relative warmth of my quarters—'quarters' might be a bit of at stretch; my quarters were a small, green, three-person tent. The journal entry for Tuesday 11 October marks the transition from being on safari to being on the mountain, and one of the most vivid recollections from that report was seeing the school children debus from the people carrier in the middle of the jungle. However, I want to reflect on my safari experience before returning to my thoughts about education in Tanzania.

In the days before cheap air travel, most of the families living on our council estate in Welwyn Garden City rarely

---

[19] I misquoted Charles Handy in my journal entry for Day 1. Handy cites an old Chinese saying that: 'Happiness is having something to do, something to hope for and someone to love', and this appears in his 2002 book *The Elephant and the Flea* p.215. Handy is an author specialising in life-lessons and I consulted his books widely before I left the Royal Air Force in 2008.

travelled abroad. Indeed, nearly all my summer holidays were spent staying with my grandmother who lived in Clydebank, Scotland. One year my family stayed in a caravan in Great Yarmouth, and we thought this trip was exotic. Like most children growing up in the 1970s, my view of Africa was shaped through television. I have already reflected on the famines in Ethiopia and the frequent Blue Peter appeals to send food and buy oxen for stricken African communities. But the other view of Africa ingrained from childhood was scenes from the wonderful wildlife programmes the BBC produced, and still produce, which Sir David Attenborough adroitly narrated from manifold properly exotic locations.

Some of Sir David's programmes reflected peaceful and tranquil settings, I particularly remember his socialising with a band of Gorillas in the mountains on the border between the Democratic Republic of Congo and Rwanda. It was the high drama of the hunt in the Serengeti that left a much greater impression on me, however. A pride of lions first stalking and then collectively bringing down a hapless wildebeest in the savanna, throwing up clouds of dust and with all the associated blood and gore of the kill; these scenes were frequent prime time viewing.

I also remember watching on television herds of stampeding antelope trying to outrun a very fast-moving cheetah, wild dogs trekking for miles to hunt down a buffalo, and leopards hunting spritely Thompson gazelles. Invariably, there was rousing music accompanying the chase scenes, followed with bitter and noisy squabbles between the victorious hunters and opportunist scavengers. Such was my concept of the African savanna before I visited, but as our party entered the Ngorongoro plain on that first Saturday spent in Africa, my first impression was one of peace and tranquillity.

There was no sound, and the animals were all mooching about nonchalantly, minding their own business. Seeing these exotic creatures in their natural habitats for the first time proved captivating and, initially, I had no cognisance of my fellow travellers—words were few. Then someone would point out a distant elephant, exotic birds, or a herd of zebra to break my reverie and the jeep would rock as we all shifted position to obtain the best view. I had seen these creatures only in cages or penned in enclosures at wildlife parks and zoos, and now it was me caged in a sturdy enclosure with these magnificent creatures gazing at me. I considered the experience to be a huge privilege, but at the same time it seemed surreal—where was the drama, the blood lust, the shrieks, the dust clouds?

I almost felt as if we could stop the jeep and set up a picnic in the middle of the grassy meadows. Then we saw them, the lions! They were beautifully camouflaged as they slept huddled together in a small gully, but not so camouflaged that a passing herd of Thompson gazelles did not notice them. Indeed, these small 'Tommies' were passing within touching distance of the sleeping lions seemingly without a care in the world. It was as if they knew the lions would not be hunting them at that time of day.

When I reviewed the safari entries in my journal, I reflected on those Thompson gazelles passing the sleeping lions in the context of the Jungle Book[20]. Although the setting for the Jungle Book is India as opposed to Africa, I considered

---

[20] *The Jungle Book*, Rudyard Kipling, first published in 1894.

that the rules of the Jungle might be the same. I recalled an idea from Rudyard Kipling's masterpiece that hunters needed permission to hunt. Happily, I still have my childhood copy to refer to and one of the chapters is entitled *Kaa's Hunting*. In the opening paragraphs of this chapter, Baloo is teaching Mowgli, the man-cub, the laws of the jungle:

*Then too, Mowgli, was taught the Strangers' Hunting Call, which must be repeated aloud till it is answered...*

*"Give me leave to hunt here because I am hungry"; and the answer is: "Hunt then, for food, but not for pleasure."*

I have never been a particular champion of animal rights, but I do not understand any human being that hunts for pleasure. I had always been uneasy about the wealthy foreigners that trek to Africa specifically to kill for enjoyment, the so-called *trophy hunters,* but since seeing these wonderful creatures for myself, the thought of humans paying to kill lions and other wild animals is abhorrent. How any human would think it okay to kill wild animals and then parade themselves for photographs next to their blooded trophies is beyond any comprehension. However, few such controversial issues are black and white; there are counterarguments in the debate.

Conservationists in Africa appeared on UK television recently to contend that the money wealthy tourists pay for the *pleasure* of killing a wild lion, for example, allows them to finance animal conservation programmes. Old, diseased, or injured wild animals that can no longer hunt successfully on the savanna might potentially terrorise farm communities or Massai Bomas to prey on domesticated goats and cattle.

Allowing wealthy tourists to kill such animals is viewed as selective culling, the proceeds of which feed back into conservation.

Another argument is that making trophy hunting illegal could make wealthy foreigners turn to poachers to achieve their desires, and without making any financial contribution to the community. This would be non-systematic or non-programmed culling that would prove more detrimental to the animal population. Some scientists argue that trophy hunting denudes the animal gene pool, while other scientists present research that shows the various gene pools benefitting from selective culling. There are no right answers, but on balance my position remains unchanged—no human should kill a wild animal in Africa for pleasure; nevertheless, I fully respect the right of the Tanzanian people to decide on their own wildlife policies, and I am resolved to be more attentive to the plight of the African wildlife and their conservation in future.

If the venerable Mr Kipling was correct, then I am guessing that on the day I visited the Ngorongoro Crater, the lions had not sought leave to hunt and thus the Thompson gazelles could pass close by unmolested. Either that, or the lions had just eaten.

# Day 2: Wednesday
# 12 October 2022

The day started early for me as I had to sortie to ease springs at about 0300. It was extraordinary because the moon was so bright it was like daylight. I could see everything and did not need my headtorch. As I write this journal, I am starting to feel the effects of hypoxia, which is also evident in the state of my handwriting. I hope I am going to be able to read this back. I have taken another garlic pill, and I might need to concede defeat and take an altitude tablet. I'll keep drinking plenty of water and just hope that I can acclimatise as the days unfold. I must reach the summit and must swallow my pride if need be and take the altitude pills.

As I write, it is about 6pm and I am already feeling the temperature starting to drop. I do not know exactly how cold it gets, but my water bottle froze last night so it most definitely is below zero—I pray to providence that I do not succumb to altitude sickness.

Today started at about 0630 when I was roused out of my warm and toasty sleeping bag. It was getting light, and I quickly clothed myself and then packed my kit. By the time the 'washy-washy'[21] water was delivered, the sun had broken over the ridge of the mountain and the warmth was instant. I stripped off again to use the water and carried out the last bit of admin so that I would be ready to move straight after breakfast. I *was* ready to move straight after breakfast, but I was the only one. Bit of soldiering, getting yourself ready to move as soon as you wake up before having breakfast.

*Gerry enjoying the last warmth of the day before layering up for the evening meal.*

---

[21] The *washy-washy* water was delivered each morning in a small orange bowl. The water was lukewarm and was only about an inch deep, but we all learned to make the most of it and were amazed at how clean we could keep ourselves with such a small amount of water.

We moved off 30 minutes late and the pace was set by *Seraphim*, our guide for the morning. It was a slow pace, not unlike the cadence for the Queen's funeral precession—and so initially the trekkers bunched up. We chatted together and spoke to the guides a bit more—they all had English names; one of the guides was called *King James*. I told him that I would bend the knee next time I saw him. The other guide with us was *Oscar*. We trekked slowly (*Pole, Pole* in Swahili); nevertheless, the party soon began to space out.

*Still a long way to go, the mountain was always somewhere in front of you on the trek.*

Later in the morning I caught up with Jennie and was taken aback when she said she had been ill—stomach pains! I could not do anything for her but tried to reassure her that all would be well as she had her man with her—Big D himself. Thankfully, she improved throughout the day and she was spared having to 'make the decision'.

We had a few stops along the way, and I chatted to different folk—they are all very interesting people. Before I set off on the trek, I had a good chat with Jim Fairlie—the brother of Andrew Fairlie, the 2-star Michelin chef that died just after Wendy had passed away and for whom we were doing this climb. I had been quite wary of Jim because he is a member of the Scottish National Party and Member of the Scottish Parliament, and I considered it a given that he must therefore hate the English. He did seem to warm to me that said when he found out that I was born in Glasgow. Nevertheless, he confided that he went into politics because he wants an independent Scotland—fair enough.

Then we spoke about the people we had lost, his brother and my wife Wendy. It proved to be a bit of a leveller and we took counsel in the loss of loved ones. Jim then asked me what Wendy was like. I had never been asked that question before and replied presently that Wendy had been my best friend and that we were nauseatingly happy together—cancer changed everything. We both ended up quite emotional. We set off on the trek knowing each other much better.

The scenery continued to give and nothing disappointed. We were heading for Cathedral Point and were told that this had been a place of human sacrifice after a bitter battle between two tribes in and around our first campsite. I was glad that Jim had found out that I was really a Scot so I might avoid being selected for sacrifice. We left our packs at the bottom of a rise we had to scramble up and I took my trekking poles out for the first time, which proved to be an incumbrance—I had never used them before and the poles I took with me had been Wendy's. It took about 30–40 minutes to reach the top where there was a sheer drop either side—the guides warned us to stay away from the edge.

The scramble was well worth it. The view was stunning, and we found ourselves looking at the top of a blanket of clouds—it felt as if you could step off and walk on them. I took some photographs and showed off my BRJ[22] running top to please the gang back home. Of course, wearing my BRJ top I have been thinking about Karen again. I keep dropping her into the conversation, especially when talking about my heritage in Clydebank and Karen's having served aboard the QE2[23].

After spending a short time at Cathedral Point, we continued to the camp, which we could already see in the distance—it was one of those cases where we seemed to walk for hours, and it never became any closer. The route passed a concrete helicopter pad, which was rather comforting because there was a road heading away from it down the mountain. I considered that the porters could not possibly carry 8 days' worth of food and water for us and them, so they must have replenishment points where food, gas, etc could be brought up.

We finally made it to the camp at about 1330 and my porter, Richard, had already pitched the tent and stowed my

---

[22] BRJ Run and Tri Club Huntingdon; BRJ are the initials of the founders.

[23] Karen had been in the merchant navy and had served aboard the Cunard liner, Queen Elizabeth 2, which my grandfather had helped to build in John Brown's shipyard in Clydebank. My mother tells me that I was at the launch in 1967.

kit therein—what a bloke. The day before, I had worn my shorts on the trek and my socks were covered in the thick tenacious volcanic dust—a deep grey colour. So, this morning I donned my long trousers and my gaiters, which proved to be a sensible move. When I arrived at the camp, Richard brushed me down to remove as much of the volcanic dust as possible. We had a cup of tea and some more 'washy-washy' before lunch.

Lunch turned out to be a 4-course meal—I am not going to lose any weight on this trip. The porters make sure that we are all well fed. After lunch, I decided that I could not avoid the 'internet café' any longer—the 'internet café' was the colloquial name for the toilet. I took a deep breath and opened the zip only to find that one of my fellow trekkers was already sat on the Elsan (bucket) with his tweeds around his ankles. Richard Mayne, or Sir Richard to his fellow trekkers, was rather shocked to say the least. I moved across to the secondary internet café and it was in a dreadful state. I will never again take the porcelain for granted.

It's quite an uncomfortable position; your buttocks are held too close together. The process seemed to go on for an age, and I was worried that the wretched thing would poke out of the top. It was a most traumatic experience. I was resolved to use the 'drop from a great height' lavatories in future or to do my business in the undergrowth.

*Note to self, I must make sure that I always have some wet wipes on me.*

Later, I apologised to Sir Richard for interrupting his constitutional, and happily he took it all in good humour.

Once we had all eaten and attended to our admin, we went back to our tents for a rest. I fell asleep straightaway. It felt like only a heartbeat when Richard, my porter, was rapping on my tent to rouse me for the acclimatisation climb. We were due to march up to 4,000m and then march back down again.

We walked up steadily—even slower than before—and eventually reached the magic 4,000m (13,000ft). I remarked that if you were flying in a non-pressurised aeroplane, you would be required to wear an oxygen mask above 10,000ft. We sang a few choruses of 'On Top of the World' by the Carpenters and Paul O'Brien treated us to a solo rendition of the second verse—most of us knew only the first verse and the chorus. Then the party repaired back to the camp. It had been only an hour's trek, but it proved exhausting.

When we made it back down, we had more washy-washy and then tea was laid on for us in the mess tent. I started to experience minor headaches and thought that I was experiencing the symptoms of altitude sickness. I wasn't the only one. There were a few trekkers missing at the dining table, including Jennie Cochrane, who had decided to go to bed early. It did not seem that long ago since we had eaten lunch, I was not very hungry—so I just picked at my food and then repaired to my tent to write up the journal. It was only 1933 and we were told that we would be roused at 0730—that would be 12 hours in the tent. I considered going out to look at the stars once I had written up the journal, but it was far too cold.

I have just returned from a sortie to the internet café, and I did pause to view the stars—amazing! I'm certain that I could see the Milky Way. There was a 'milky' white band running north to south amongst the stars—I am no astronomer, but I'm going to claim that I have seen the Milky Way. As I suspected, it is bloody cold and despite wearing my long johns, heavy trousers, 2 pairs of socks, base layer, fleece and Mammut jacket, I started shivering.

When my mum told me that she had knitted a scarf to take with me to Africa, I thought: '*ah bless her.*' To be honest, though, it has been an absolute Godsend—I'm wearing it now. I feel a bit like Scott of the Antarctic at the moment as I'm huddled up in the tent with my legs inside my sleeping bag, writing my journal. Luckily, we are super well fed and so far, no injuries to contend with—touch wood.

Earlier in the evening when I complained of headaches, I took 2 of my garlic pills (thanks Jo Watts[24]), and as I write now—it's still only 2020—my headache has abated. I'm going to keep taking these pills. I'm taking my anti-malaria tablets too, even though there are no mosquitoes up here, and my Vitamin B[25] (thanks Karen), *even though there are no mosquitoes up here*. I am also remembering to take my statin. We were told to leave our books behind, but I so wish that I had a novel with me—what am I going to do for another 11 hours cooped up in this tent?

---

[24] Jo Watts is one of my friends from the running club and she had experienced altitude sickness in some of her adventures. She advocated taking garlic pills as they increased the red blood cells' ability to absorb oxygen and thus counter the effects of altitude sickness. It did seem to work for me as I never had to take any of the prescribed pills.

[25] Owing to her experiences serving on cruise ships, Karen had been widely travelled and she recommended taking Vitamin B to counter mosquito bites—again this regime appeared to work as I survived in Africa for nearly two weeks without incurring any bites.

I have been very pleased with my solar-powered battery pack. It charged the smartphone no bother, and quickly charged itself up after only a short while in the morning Kilimanjaro sun. I suppose one option would be to read one of the novels downloaded on to my smartphone Kindle before dropping off. So, here I am at the end of Day 2 on the mountain (Wednesday 12 October 2022)—how am I feeling?

I have been talking a lot about my experiences as a lecturer and all the wonderful people I met during that time. I recounted some of the stories of how people (my students) had changed their lives through education and how I had helped them to realise their ambitions. I think that perhaps I quit the Open University too soon, but I have no inkling to go back to lecturing. I am sort of enjoying my work with the Royal Aeronautical Society[26], but it is not entirely satisfying or financially worthwhile.

I also have no inkling to go back to contracting—I could not bear the thought of having to engage with rules, regulations and disagreeable regulators. The prospect of working for an NGO[27] occurred to me, and this has certainly been more in my thoughts during my time in Africa, but the notion of being away from home for months on end does not appeal to me either.

Moreover, I am not sure that the manifold NGOs that are already active in Africa and the rest of the world are doing any good at all—are we simply trying to impose our values

---

[26] After my cruise in April 2022, I started working freelance for the Royal Aeronautical Society assessing graduates and ex-apprentices for professional recognition from the Engineering Council.

[27] Non-Government Organisation.

on people that should be left to develop at their own pace? I keep coming back to the one thing I can reasonably achieve and potentially leave behind and that is writing. I must therefore get myself into a position where I write as a profession—maybe I could also consider leaving the Willows[28]. No, I hesitated even as I wrote that last sentence. I can't leave the Willows—not yet anyway.

*I'm going to take my meds before writing anymore—meds duly taken.*

So where has my idle musing left me? At the risk of sounding like Lizz Truss: Writing, Writing, Writing! What about my love life? It has been a bit rocky and largely heart breaking, but I have had a lot of fun with Karen. Who knows where it will lead, but I should keep going and see what happens.

That's it for tonight—Day 3 to look forward to tomorrow. I'm getting up at 0730 and then we are walking for only 2 hours to the next camp. Once there, we go for more acclimatisation. These small treks are sure to be crucial to the success of my mission.

\*\*\*

By the second day of the climb, I had really started to bond with my fellow trekkers. Although they were mostly all working in hospitality, they were a very diverse and eclectic

---

[28] The Willows is the name of the house where I live in Cambridgeshire.

group of people. Callum McNally had just been elected to his local council and was about to start working full-time for the Scottish Labour Party. We very politely exchanged a few political views and generally we were in lockstep about the seemingly appalling state of the country. I was very encouraging towards Callum and told him that I was pleased to see younger people taking an interest in politics. I had no doubt that Callum was entering politics for all the right reasons, and I wished him all the very best with his endeavours. As one of the few English people amongst a group of Scots, I generally eschewed political discourse.

At this stage in the expedition, I was wary of talking to Jim Fairlie, whom as I already mentioned was serving in the Scottish Parliament as a member of the Scottish National Party (SNP). The SNP is hardly known throughout the world for being anglophiles, and I considered that my being an English unionist would mean that Jim and I would have very little in common. As my journal records, our first conversations were indeed about UK politics and Jim vehemently but politely stated his position. In true *Desiderata* fashion, I spoke my own truth quietly and clearly, and Jim listened before reinforcing his argument with some examples of how frustrating the current setup had been for him.

For my own part, I had long been disenfranchised with politics; for many years I felt that no political party represented my views, or could pursue a simple, common-sense, balanced approach to running the country. I had been greatly ashamed of the seeming incompetence of government, and the reprehensible behaviour of our politicians at Westminster. Moreover, I was embarrassed that their unashamed, immature approach to debating in parliament was being broadcast around the world. I therefore had some sympathy for the Scottish people that wished to divorce themselves from Westminster and I quipped to Jim Fairlie that if I had the opportunity, I would divorce myself from Westminster too.

When I confided my reflections to Jim, he was rather disappointed that I had seemingly been left with the impression that he was anti-English and warmed to me only when he found out I had been born in Scotland. I did not return from the expedition with anything like that impression, but it was churlish of me to even hint that Jim was anti-English without revisiting my musings on the Mountain. Moreover, it was disingenuous of me to equate Scottish Nationalism with anti-Englishness in the first place. Jim confided that his desire for independence is about the right to self-determination and that his passion is pro-Scottish as opposed to being anti anything.

I had joined the Royal Air Force (RAF) as an engineer officer, but very early in my career I entered the regular process of staff training, which included a large element of defence studies. Defence studies would be more aptly named 'war studies' because the whole point of military training is to prepare for war. I believed in the maxim that being prepared for war made war less likely; but as I have observed over the years, this maxim does not necessary hold true in practice. Indeed, to echo Ehrmann's view of love, it would be fair to observe that war is as perennial as the grass too.

I remember delivering my first defence studies speech on what was then called the Junior Officers' Command Course— JOCC, which seems rather apt given the large proportion of 'jocks' climbing Kilimanjaro with me. I stood up in front of my peers, superior officers, and some wizened academics from Kings College London who were charged with teaching junior officers the nuances of critical thought. Although nervous, I asserted loudly and aggressively that the roots of war boiled down to division, plain and simple. Division between groups of human beings at many different levels; nation states, communities, religions, and I even spoke about football teams.

My pitch was that my brother and I were several years apart at school and ended up supporting rival football teams in north London, I expressed that whenever these teams clashed in a league match, he and I would be on different sides of the football stadium. Nevertheless, when the England team were playing, he and I would be stood together in the stadium. My pitch for a more peaceful world was therefore to *simply* breakdown the divisions.

I cringe at my naivety in those early career days, and, happily, my approach to such complex topics has matured. The effect of divisions in society and in the international community cannot be treated lightly, however, and the investigation and analysis of divisions feature prominently whenever NGO's and militaries design intervention programmes. Investigating the topic, as part of my lecturing role, I discovered another approach to global peace-making that my trip to Kilimanjaro prompted me to reflect upon.

In her book, *Do No Harm*[29], Mary Anderson collates manifold different and wide-ranging experiences of providing aid in civil war and other conflict scenarios to understand how aid and conflict interact. She argues that although many

---

[29] *Do No Harm*, Mary B Anderson, Lynne Rienner Publishers, 1999.

NGO's are well intentioned, they end up doing harm and one of the reasons cited was a lack of contextual understanding. Academics consider *Nightingale's Risk* where well-meaning agencies such as *Medicines sans Frontier* (MSF) provide medical aid to combatants in civil war theatres. Nightingale's Risk, named after Florence Nightingale, the Lady of the Lamp in the military hospitals during the Crimean War, considers that if the warring factions do not have to look after their wounded or displaced people, they are less likely to end the fighting.

After years of research in conflict areas all over the globe, a pattern began to emerge, which Anderson rationalised into a framework for analysing the impact of aid on conflict in terms of dividers and *connectors* qualified in different categories.

Anderson observed that even in the most bitterly fought and most atrocious civil war scenarios, there were more people not involved in killing their neighbours than were doing so. More societies avoid warfare than engage in it. More would-be leaders fail to arouse people to violence than succeed in doing so and that even in today's troubled world, peace is more widespread than war[30].

When I reflect on my first one-to-one conversation with Jim Fairlie at the start of our adventure, we were hugely divided—English Unionist meets Scottish Nationalist, the potential for heated discourse or mutual aversion was manifold. Jim may disagree, but on that beautiful morning on the slopes of Mount Kilimanjaro, we found that our grieving for the loved ones we had lost was an experience we both

---

[30] Ibid, p.24

shared, a connection. Later the shared experience of our adventure would strengthen this connection, not only with Jim, but also with my fellow trekkers.

Since Anderson published her research in 1999, the world appears to have become much more volatile, and I wonder whether her assertions still hold true. Russia invaded Ukraine early in 2022 and in 2023, war has broken out between Israel and Hamas in the Gaza Strip after Hamas terrorists carried out a breathtakingly brutal incursion in southern Israel. Since we returned from Africa in October 2022, there have been several coups including 2 in Burkina Faso and takeovers in Niger, Guinea Bissau, the Gambia, Sao Tome and Principe, Guinea, Mali and Chad—most of which were nascent democracies.

The worrying thing is that the UK public appears indifferent to the resurgence of dictatorships in Africa and warfare in general. Indeed, in September 2023, many ethnic Armenians were killed or displaced when the Azerbaijan Army ethnically cleansed the disputed region of Nagorno Karabakh, and our news bulletins at the time were dominated by allegations of sexual misconduct against the comedian Russell Brand, whoever he is! It takes a huge leap of faith to believe Anderson's assertion that peace is more widespread than war; nevertheless, we must hope that the connections in civil society prevail.

# Day 3: Thursday 13 October 2022

I have just had my second go on the Elsan (internet café) and this attempt proved much better and more successful than the first time—but rest assured I will never get used to it and will always value the porcelain. I have just taken a couple more garlic capsules. I figured that it would be impossible to overdose on garlic so I'm taking about 6 per day—they appear to be working.

I am keeping myself clean but keeping my kit clean is extremely difficult. The mountain is so dusty, and it is a dark tenacious dust that clings to everything. My porter, Richard, sweeps me down at the end of every walk so that I can take my gaiters and boots off without putting dust everywhere. He will be expecting a big tip at the end of the trek[31].

Today was a short walk to Camp 3, which was about 4,220m above sea level. We arrived there about 1100 and dumped our packs for an acclimatisation climb to around 4,600m, which is said to be the height of Camp 4. We climbed up to a rocky outcrop that reminded me of the mountains in

---

[31] I was being churlish towards Richard in my journal. He never had any expectation of a reward from me of any kind, he was simply a very genuine hardworking bloke keen to do his very best for me.

Monument Valley, Arizona. Some of the trekkers quipped that it was more like Wylie Coyote territory from the cartoon Roadrunner. The climb was tough, and I was glad I dumped my pack. We climbed very slowly, but still there were trekkers dragging behind. Nevertheless, we all made it to the top and there was a great deal of positive mental attitude around the camp. It is painfully slow, that said, as all walking ceased at 1330 today and we won't be on the march again until 0830 tomorrow morning. I have been reading about the run-up to the First World War on my smartphone Kindle, but I so wish I had brought my novel with me. At least I will have it for the flight home.

I am missing home. I miss snuggling up with Poppy[32] and watching Netflix, especially *Big Bang Theory* and I miss the Willows. I am so glad to be here in Africa and I will make it to the top of Mount Kilimanjaro, but I think this will be my last adventure of this sort. Of course, there are still many places I would like to see in the world, but I will do so from the comfort of a decent hotel.

I had a very pleasant night in the tent last night; I slept for long periods and was awake a few times. During one of my waking periods, I started reading the smartphone Kindle. It was a bit tricky reading from inside the sleeping bag, but it was not as cold last night as it had been on the first night, so I could put my head and arms out of the bag. I decided to use my piss pot for the first time as I did not fancy going outside. It was quite nerve-wracking as I did not want to overfill the bottle and I was listening to the tone in the same way that you do when you fill a glass from a tap. It passed without incident.

---

[32] Poppy is my cat.

I am very pleased that the guides know what they are doing. We are being broken in easily and made to do acclimatisation treks with long rests in between. I really like my trekking mates too; there is guy called Roddy who keeps the camp going with his dour Scottish jokes. My favourite Roddy joke is the one about a Scottish couple. The husband says to his wife: "I'm aff tae the pub, get yer hat and coat."

The wife replies: "Am I coming with yee?"

"Naw," says the husband, "I'm turning the heating aff!"

After the long lie-downs this afternoon, we were mustered at about 1600 for tea and cake. It was still quite warm, and I changed into my pre-dinner dress of fleece and heavy trousers. I have discovered that I like tea with a spoonful of honey in it. I really do not like the powdered milk provided in the mess, so I thought I would have my tea black. The honey here is much runnier than mine at home. I find I like tea and honey a lot and there is less caffeine content compared with that of the coffee, which means I sleep better.

After tea and cake, Sophia—she is on our trek, but lives in Tanzania (she is originally from Denmark)—arranged a mindfulness session where we formed a ring of stones and sat around meditating and exercising our breathing. The final exercise involved ridding the body of tension and headache—I found the exercise very relaxing, and the surroundings were spectacular. I have read about Buddhist mindfulness before and have tried to meditate a few times without much success, but Sophia's session was tremendous.

I generally feel okay. I don't have any of the altitude sickness symptoms I experienced on Day 1 (I think the garlic works). I do find that I become breathless quickly if I overexert… well, exert at any level. The tortoise wins the race here and everything must be done slowly—even writing. For anyone reading this journal in the future, I am writing on my knee as there are no desks and chairs in the tent. I also think that the altitude is affecting my brain and it's more difficult to write neatly. That's why I must take the journal writing slowly too.

We are sleeping in 3-man tents, but there are only 2 of us—Karl Mitchell and me. This means that we can put our kitbags in the middle. I haven't slept on the floor of a small tent for many years, and I have surprised myself at how well I have adapted. You do need to be organised though and know where everything is. It is also a good idea to stow the sleeping bag as soon as you get up so that you can create some room to organise your kit. I find it takes me less and less time, and I can be up, packed, and ready to move in less than 30 minutes. Despite my newfound, or rediscovered, camping skills, I am resolved to stay in a decent hotel when I travel henceforth. I have proved myself 'hardcore' and will leave the rough and tough to the youngsters.

I noticed when we were meditating that the porters were singing their traditional African songs. It reminded me of the film *Zulu*, where all the Zulus are chanting in front of the British soldiers at Rourke's Drift. I knew that I was going to be cold on Kilimanjaro, but I thought we would be cold only near the summit. The temperature range throughout the day is huge. It starts frosty and then for most of the afternoon, I am comfortable in a tee-shirt and sunhat with factor 50 on my exposed arms. Once the sun sets, I must don long johns, heavy trousers, a fleece, two pairs of socks and my Mammut jacket.

So, how do I feel at the end of Day 3? I feel fit and I have a very positive mental attitude. But I am also feeling positive about my future—I cannot wait to get on with it.

***

In 2011, I was working for the UK Ministry of Defence in the Lockheed Tristar[33] Project Team. A serving RAF squadron leader, Jim Riddell, approached me and asked if I still had my No.1 Uniform (Best Blue) and, if so, did it still fit. Somewhat confused about the question I replied that my old uniform was undoubtedly hanging in the wardrobe somewhere but given the noticeable increase in my body mass index since leaving the RAF, I doubted very much whether my old blue suit would still fit. He quickly explained that they were looking for someone to bash the bass drum in the RAF Wyton Voluntary Band.

I dismissed the notion because I had never been a musician, but Jim insisted that I would be up to the task—allegedly, bashing the bass drum was straightforward and did not require any music skill. Seemingly, the only criteria I had to meet was owning an RAF uniform that fitted. I dusted off my old uniform and readily discovered that my enlarged civilian girth disqualified me at the first hurdle; so that should have been the end of it, but providence appeared to suggest otherwise.

I met the Bandmaster and frapped my way around the gymnasium at RAF Wyton. A former Irish Guardsman, the

---

[33] Lockheed L1011 Tristar was a wide-bodied commercial airliner that the RAF converted for military use in 1984.

Bandmaster confided the basic requirements and signals, and with the loan of an RAF uniform that fitted perfectly, I was enlisted into the band. It turned out that you did have to have some music skill—beating the drum at a steady 116 beats per minute, for one thing! Initially, I tended to speed up during the march, which would require my hapless bandmates to 'jog' around Huntingdonshire. Nevertheless, I eventually became a half decent bass drummer and along with my side drummers, we became known as Gerry and the Pacemakers.

In 2015, the band was playing in St Paul's Cathedral to mark the 75th anniversary of the Battle of Britain. Jeremy Corbin had recently been elected as leader of the Labour Party and he was attending the service in this capacity. He immediately caused controversy when he refused to sing the national anthem, and my claim to fame is that it was our band that was playing the national anthem at the time—I did the rolls at the start of the piece alongside the other Pacemakers. But this occasion was memorable for another more important reason—it was the event that inspired me to become a 'real' musician.

A wonderful musician from our band, her name was Marina, played a solo on her tenor horn for a piece entitled, 'An Elegy on the RAF March Past'[34]. Instead of the 116 beats per minute, this most iconic march is played slowly and mournfully, and it was especially beautiful played in the setting of St Paul's Cathedral. I was so moved that 3 years later a recording of our band performing the Elegy was played at Wendy's funeral; this seemed the most perfect way to honour a woman that had either been in the RAF or married

---

[34] Elegy (On an RAF Theme) H B Hingley (1994).

to it for most of her life. Marina inspired me to become a 'true' musician, and I enrolled in the Huntingdonshire Music School to learn to play the saxophone. Music has been a huge part of my life ever since; indeed, playing music as part of a band or orchestra makes me happy and has comforted me through some difficult experiences.

I found learning to play an instrument in my late 40s incredibly challenging. Desiderata entreats us to *Take kindly the counsel of the years, gracefully surrendering the things of youth.* On more than one occasion, even now, I considered learning to play an instrument a thing of youth that I should gracefully surrender. One day I was lamenting my struggle to the Rector at our parish church when he inspired me with a simple maxim. The Rector confided that music was in fact a gift from God and whenever you play, no matter how skilled or otherwise, you were making the world a little better. I did wonder if the Rector would stand by this maxim if he heard me playing; nevertheless, I took his words to heart and I reflect on them whenever I think about the Kilimanjaro porters singing away on those frosty mornings and throughout the day as they carried their enormous loads to the next camp.

The porters' lives are incredibly hard. They roused themselves before dawn, tended to our every need as we slowly emerged from our little green tents. Then they would pack up the camps and carry everything, including our personal kit, over miles of rocky and dusty terrain to set up the camp again before we arrived. They were always cheerful and were always singing and hearing them certainly made our lives a little better.

Indeed, music, in my view, could be considered a super-connector. Having struggled to learn to read music, I know that I could probably go anywhere in the world and be able to play in an orchestra even if I did not understand the spoken language. Music connects us to our past, to loved ones, to happy times and sad times. It nurtures the spirit, calms the soul, and motivates us to achieve seemingly untenable challenges—like climbing the highest free-standing mountain in the world.

I also reflect on how important music was to Wendy. One day when I was in our living room struggling to play a simple piece from my Abracadabra Saxophone book[35], she asked to have a go. After a cursory wipe of the reed, she played the piece I had been struggling with, note-perfect, and was exceedingly pleased with herself. I remarked that I had no idea she could play the saxophone and she replied that she had never played one in her life. "Oh really?" I quipped with as much sarcasm as I could muster.

She had played the clarinet in a youth orchestra when she was at school and, as she so eloquently proved, the skills required to play the clarinet allowed her to play the saxophone. When she succumbed to cancer a second time, the family chipped in to buy Wendy a new clarinet and she was able to play some of her favourite tunes to reconnect her with happier times. I soon realised that playing the saxophone does not necessarily mean you can play the clarinet, so Wendy's clarinet has rested silently in its case since she passed away. Perhaps it is time for Wendy's clarinet to sing again.

I was hugely impressed that the funds raised from our climb to the top of Mount Kilimanjaro would be used to train

---

[35] Abracadabra Saxophone Alto: The Way to Learn Through Songs and Tunes, Johnathan Rutland, Collins (2008) ISBN: 140107635.

young people to become artisans in the hospitality industry. I wondered whether I could create a scholarship of my own to teach disadvantaged yet talented children to play the clarinet.

I mentioned this idea to my music teacher when I resumed lessons after my trip to Africa, and she said that she would be happy to support the scholarship and that we would teach suitable candidates to play Wendy's clarinet. Moreover, if this proved successful, we could widen the scholarship to other children and other instruments. The seed was planted.

# Day 4: Friday 14 October 2022

The battle rhythm was pretty much the same as yesterday. Reveille was at 0630 and I was up, packed, dressed, and ready to move by 0700—the Party did not move until 0845. As we get closer to the summit, we are increasingly in the shadow of it. We are on the western side of Mount Kilimanjaro, so it takes the sun longer to crest the top of the mountain every day. I am writing up today's journal entries with the tent open as the sun sets behind the lava tower. It is truly spectacular, and the photos on my smartphone simply do not do the scenery justice. Just as I wrote that, the porter rapped at the tent and said that dinner was ready.

It was very nice tonight: stir fry beef, rice and vegetable sauce.

We had the brief for tomorrow, but I shall return to that after I have recorded the events of today. The whole point of the long trek to the summit is to train our bodies for the final assault. For 4 days now, we have marched to camp, rested, then climbed to a greater altitude before returning to the camp. Today was especially tough as the camp is at 4300m and we climbed to 4900m. Many of the trekkers felt the pain and some were sick on the climb. One poor fellow, Craig, had to stay behind as he was not coping with the altitude at all well.

I gave him some of my garlic pills, but I think the damage was already done.

Amanda was tearful when we made it to the top, she had really struggled. We are so high that you get breathless putting your boots on—so when you are climbing, it is literally one foot in front of the other. Climbing is painfully slow, but it must be. We saw our first ice today and it was melting under the heat of the sun, and this meant that we had to cross a small stream. The most difficult thing to do is dress correctly to cope with the range of temperatures. I keep to the mantra, *be bold: start cold*, because it soon warms up on the climb. However, it only needs a bank of cloud to move in and the temperature drops. Then the clouds part and you're too hot; further on you cross a ridge, the wind picks up, it gets cold again, and so on.

I am sat fully clothed with my feet in the sleeping bag and I can feel the temperature dropping. It is 2000 (8pm), and I will take some layers off shortly to make a pillow before tucking myself into the bag—it is my old military surplus arctic sleeping bag and even after 30 years it keeps me toasty.

Today's climb was up to Lava Tower Camp. It was a spectacular tower, which bears down ominously on the camp below. We arrived at about midday and the tents were already set up as always, and Richard was there to brush me down as always. I had my photo taken with him at the camp sign—he is a real gem. I have decided that I am going to try to clear my system before I take my layers off as I really do not fancy having to sortie from the tent to ease springs tonight. It is already dark, and the stars are amazing; however, you must not tarry too long outside the tents to look at them as you soon start to shiver. Come to Africa and freeze your backside off!

After lunch, we had a long lie-down and then we conducted the acclimatisation climb. The guide told us that the gradient was the same as we could expect on the final assault, so it was good training.

*The Author, Jennie and Big D posing together at the base of the Lava Tower.*

So here I am at the end of Day 4, how do I feel? I think I am mending my bridges with Jennie and David; I think they were mended already, but this trip is serving to reinforce the bridge, and I am very grateful for the opportunity. Jennie asked me if I was glad to have rejoined the expedition. I said that I was very glad to have been invited to rejoin—so the bridges to build part of the expedition was going well. This is certainly one of the most challenging, hardcore things I have ever done, and I am increasingly confident that I will reach the top—positive mental attitude! Would I do it again? Not on your Nelly!

*The Author with his personal porter, Richard, at the Lava Tower Camp on Day 4 of the trek.*

Emotionally, I think I'm doing okay. I think a lot about Karen all the time and cannot wait to see her again. There was a glimmer of a 4G signal in the camp and I tried to message her. Whether she receives the message or not in is the lap of the phone gods. But if I play my cards right, there should be lots of fun to be had once I get home.

\*\*\*

I am so pleased to be reconnected with Jennie and Big D. In the spring of 2023, they came to see me at the Willows and my son, Joe, came home from Norwich to spend some time with his auntie and uncle. Such a gathering would have been very difficult before the Kilimanjaro expedition, and it was such a shame that my strong desire to be connected to another individual, my former girlfriend, meant that connections with other people I loved would become so strained. Such is the nature of the human spirit that it would be impossible for everyone you are connected to in life to all be friends with each other, but this is not the main thing that comes to mind as I reflect on the events of Day 4.

My journal entry makes clear that I would never consider climbing Mount Kilimanjaro again. When the Cochrane's came to Cambridgeshire to visit, we recounted our wonderful experiences in Tanzania to such an extent that we all quipped, why wouldn't we want to climb the mountain again? Indeed, Joe was so enthralled that he insisted we go back to Tanzania so that he can climb the mountain with us. I am certainly not qualified to make assertions about the workings of the human mind, but in my experience most people have selective memories that tend to block out or minimise bad experiences.

We make light of hardships and amplify good times—this probably explains nostalgia, when we always seem to believe that things in general were a lot better in the past. The truth behind such phenomena is arguably much more complex, but another perspective is that we naturally prefer to reflect on good times and reflection serves to reinforce knowledge and experiences. Maybe this is another reason that contemporary pedagogy[36] extols the virtues of reflection. But does this really explain why I now want to go back to Mount Kilimanjaro, when my journal completely discounts any possibility of a return?

Reflection, or Reflective Practice, in the academic context is much more than reinforcing knowledge and experience, it is a process for continuous learning. I found a copy of *Reflective Practitioners* by Donald Schon[37] on my bookshelf that I referred to from time to time during my career as an associate lecturer, mostly to impress my students. Schön describes reflective practice as critically analysing an experience and recording how the experience impacted you and what you plan to do with the knowledge and insights gained. Schön's ideas have developed particularly in teaching, healthcare, and social work as a means of learning from real-life experiences. This ability to learn through reflection is fascinating.

The Cambridge University website extols the virtues of reflective practice in academic writing and builds on Schön's ideas for organisational learning. It suggests that the key to

---

[36] Pedagogy, 'the method and practice of teaching'.

[37] The Reflective Practitioner: How Professionals Think in Action, Donal A Schön, Routledge (1991).

reflection is to be analytical rather than descriptive, and to always ask why rather than just describing what happened. In my Kilimanjaro journal, I often write about how I am feeling, but I never consider why I am feeling the way I do.

It is relatively easy to understand why I felt the way I did when I was writing my journal in the confines of the small green tent. I was uncomfortable and cold, I felt unclean, I had no basic comforts like a porcelain toilet, and I had been unwell and disconnected from my friends and family. At the end of Day 4, I knew that I would still have to endure more of the same and perhaps even worse before I reached the summit— of course I would not want to endure such hardship again! Conversely, when I was reminiscing about our adventure with Jennie and David last spring, we were talking about the beauty of the Ngorongoro Crater, the African wildlife, and, when we were on the mountain, *the sense of mutual endeavour and achievement.*

When I joined the RAF in the winter of 1989, my basic training at RAF Cranwell was replete with more severe hardships compared to those I faced on Kilimanjaro. I was often uncomfortable, cold, and wet; I was detached from friends and family for months on end—there were no mobile phones in 1989—I was deprived of sleep, woken at 5am to prepare my kit for parade in the dark at 6am, or even earlier if we were being collectively punished, and then subjected to the verbal pummelling of the drill sergeants on the parade square.

These drill sergeants were unconcerned about endearing themselves to officer cadets and were apt to throw our kit out in the corridor of the barrack blocks if any of it was not presented to the drill sergeants' exacting standards. We lived in constant fear of being back coursed because we did not meet the required standards; or worse still, chopped completely because the RAF did not want us. Early in 1990, basic training culminated in the passing out parade, which turned out to be one of the proudest and happiest days of my life. I marched onto the parade square as an officer cadet with all the colleagues I had trained with and together we marched off the parade square as commissioned officers.

Whenever I meet up with any of my former Cranwell muckers (an increasingly rare occurrence after such a long time), we reminisce fondly about our time there, and it is not the fact that we have forgotten the hardships, it is quite the opposite. The hardships are part of the story, part of the achievement. We all came through it together and the upshot was that we have an almost unique bond that will be forever regarded as *the time of our lives*. The hardships we endured during our basic training made the ultimate achievement of passing out as commissioned officers so much more joyous.

I contrast this happy reminiscence with my last trip to the dentist to have 2 teeth extracted. I well remember the pain and discomfort and I know that I will still remember this pain the next time I am sat in the waiting room; indeed, I have no wish to revisit the dentist for any treatment. This is an enduring memory that has most definitely not been selectively culled! So, why do the hardships experienced on Mount Kilimanjaro no longer deter me from going back? Could it be that it is not selective memory that downplays hard times, but that the memories of happy times, especially those derived from hardship and camaraderie, are simply more powerful? Speaking personally, I believe that happiness associated with mutual endeavour and achievement, under difficult and challenging conditions, lasts a lifetime.

At the end of Day 4 on Mount Kilimanjaro, we were a long way from experiencing the joy of reaching the summit. Moreover, apart from those that had climbed the mountain before, we had no inkling of how we would all feel at the summit—so it is understandable that the prevailing view was 'never again'!

# Day 5: Saturday 15 October 2022

This was the most brutal day of the expedition so far. I had a good first sleep last night, but after I had my first pee, I doubled up with stomach cramps. I had some water and they eased enough to get some second-cycle sleep, but I had to go to the internet café at 0530 for, well, a bit of diarrhoea, which was most unpleasant sat on the Elson. I took a diarrhoea pill and at reveille I stowed my sleeping bag and packed my kit. It seemed like an age before we set off, and we had been told to expect a tough day. We had to climb the Barranco Wall, and it was almost a sheer cliff that we needed to scramble up—we collapsed our poles and put gloves on as the rocks were reported as being quite sharp—this was excellent advice.

The climb was a real slog and took most of the morning. Some of the trekkers were forced to handover their packs to the guides who were already laden with their own kit. Naturally, the slower members of the party began to drop back, and they subsequently divided into 2 groups—the first of the slow group made it back 2 hours after we arrived at the next camp; the second of the slow group has yet to arrive and we have already discussed the options for getting them to the summit. The slower group(s) are the ones that have struggled throughout the trip, but their resilience and determination have been inspiring.

Personally, I do not know how I managed to get through the day. On the march up to the wall, I was in a sort of trance. I felt very lightheaded, and Barry was talking to me, but I did not know what he was saying. Even after I cleared my ears (we were descending), I still could not register what he was saying to me. I hope Barry did not think that I was being rude.

*The towering Barranco Wall, one of the toughest and most technical parts of the trek.*

When we arrived at the base of the wall, I was a broken man. I had no idea how I was going to get over the Barranco Wall. Help presented itself in the form of a Trek bar, which is a protein bar especially formulated for trekkers—the clue is in the name. Chomping on this bar gave me a new lease of life and I really enjoyed the scramble thereafter. It was exhausting. There were many technical spots and a severe section where you had to squeeze around a ledge called the kissing stone because you literally had to kiss the stone wall to avoid falling.

I forgot to mention, it has been raining today. Nothing heavy but our party has been walking inside clouds all day. Roddy was on form and asked us what the difference was between a rolling stone and a Scottish sheep-farmer. A rolling stone says: "Hey! You! Get off of my cloud"; whereas a Scottish sheep-farmer says: "Hey! McCloud! Get off of my Ewe!" Very funny!

At the top of the wall, we gathered around a flat spot and ate our packed lunches—I wasn't hungry and just picked at mine. The guides dished out some soup, which was a delightful treat at the top of the wall, and we all felt that the hike to it and the scramble up was the hardest day's climbing we had done so far. Seemingly, we had ended up on a different side of the mountain where the flora and fauna had all changed. The slopes were filled with prehistoric looking trees and there was thick heather and some sort of daisy-type flower clumped around the slopes in abundance.

Also, there was noticeable birdsong. We have seen pigeons and big birds, which I believed were called collared ravens at the other camps, but I certainly had not heard much birdsong. I so enjoyed hearing it as we moved up and down in the clouds. The downward paths were punishing on the knees, and the upward parts punishing on the calves and hips. I did not see much of the scenery because I was just focusing on the heels in front of me and putting one foot in front of the other. I tried not to look up as there always appeared to be a horrific climb in front of us, but with one foot in front of the other, *pole-pole*, slowly, we eventually conquered the Barranco Wall.

We were at Karanga Camp now, which is 3,995m above sea level. The camp is on a slope and as reported we are in the clouds. I had a full wash in 30mm of cold water and changed my socks and underwear—it's a great feeling when you are all warm again after a cold wash. The time is 1700 and there is still no sign of our missing pair. They are in good hands, but they are likely to be exhausted. Karl, my tent buddy, asked me what I did for a living. I had already told him, I think, but I explained again how I assess young engineers for professional recognition on behalf of the Royal Aeronautical Society. It's okay as jobs go, but it is all done online; I need more interaction with people, and I might have to look around for something else when I get home. The job is not very demanding and brings in a bit of money, which should tide me over until I find something better to do.

The final pair have just returned to the camp, and they appear in good shape. Toby is still having problems with his boots. The terrain is very punishing on your footwear, and I am not likely to get mine shining again after this trip. I've just checked them over having seen Toby's boots and mine appear to be in good condition.

So, all the climbers have just been fed—beef stroganoff and noodles with fruit salad for afters. I never cease to be amazed at what the chefs can produce considering that everything needs to be carried up the mountain by the porters. We had the brief for tomorrow as well. Reveille at 0700 to head for basecamp no later than 0830. This was forecast to be a steep climb, and none of us was looking forward to it. Then

we are essentially going to bed as we must be up at midnight for the final climb to the peak. The idea is that we reach Stella Point on the rim of the old crater in time to watch the sunrise. I cannot wait; not to see the sunrise per se, but to get off this bloody mountain. I am glad I came and I would not have missed it for the world, but I miss my home comforts even more. Real porcelain in the toilets and a proper bed and being able to put my trousers on standing up. Hardcore projects best left to the youngsters now.

At the end of Day 5, how do I feel? One word—exhausted!

\*\*\*

I well remember the ups and downs of Day 5 both in terms of elevation and emotion. Notwithstanding my lack of mountain training before going to Tanzania, I believed myself to be quite fit. After all, I was an active member of an excellent running club, and I had taken part in several half-marathons and a whole host of smaller scale running events, such as the annual 10km Race for Life in aid of Cancer Research UK. It had not always been thus, however. While I had maintained a high level of fitness during my time in the RAF, I had steadily 'let myself go' in the years that followed. I was working away from home a great deal and staying in hotels.

I would indulge in a full English breakfast every morning on the premise that doing so would allow me to skip lunch, and then I would end up not skipping lunch. With a 3-course meal in the evenings followed by a huge measure of the local brew, and not a great deal of time—if any—given over to

101

fitness, my BMI[38] increased, but at such a steady rate that I did not notice how portly I had become. More alarmingly, I had entered the realms of Type-2 diabetes, a particularly disturbing revelation given that my uncle had recently died of a diabetes-related condition. I was in denial about my deteriorating health, but I was to be rudely awakened towards the end of 2017.

As I mentioned in previous reflections, I joined the RAF Wyton Voluntary Band in 2011 and had become proficient at pounding the base drum 116 times a minute for parades—*Gerry and the Pacemakers*. By the end of 2017, I had played saxophone in the concert band, but the Bandmaster would not relieve me from my tub-thumping duties—no one else appeared willing to replace me. In 2018, the massed Voluntary Bands of the Royal Air Force were due to perform a key role in the celebrations to mark the 100th anniversary of the formation of the RAF (qualified as RAF100) and I was selected to play the bass drum. We were due to march in London along the Mall from Wellington Barracks to Admiralty Arch and back to position and retrieve the route-liners[39], before and after the main parade. We practiced marching the parade distance on a cold and frosty morning at RAF Cosford in Staffordshire, and much to my shame I could

---

[38] Body Mass Index, a crude indication of your state of health derived from weight and height. Before joining Band on the Run, my BMI was gusting towards 30 (overweight); it now sits between 22–23 (healthy weight).

[39] Route liners are armed sentries—mostly young RAF recruits in this instance—that march out ahead of the main parade and are spaced out at intervals to guard the route.

not keep up the pace for the whole distance. I had to be relieved for the march back—I was devastated.

Tony Reeves, a former squadron leader in the RAF and one of my best friends, was part of the Pacemakers that day and was stood alongside me frapping his side drum. He too felt the strain of such a long march, but he already had a plan. Tony and his wife Alison, another musician, had formed some of the RAF Wyton band members into a park run[40] team, which he dubbed 'Band on the Run'. I was invited to join and ran my first ever park run on 6 January 2018.

It was a while before I did my next park run because I pulled about 5 different muscles, but that first park run changed my life. Once fit again and remembering to warm up and actuate my muscles properly, a friendly rivalry struck up between Tony and I, and we steady improved our times. One Saturday morning Tony would be out in front smashing his personal best and leaving me for dust, and a few Saturdays later I would have upped my game and would beat Tony to the finish funnel. When the RAF100 parade took place in July 2018, I had no problem frapping my base drum proudly up and down the Mall; I did not miss a beat, and what a hugely proud and happy day that turned out to be.

Sadly, Tony injured himself running a few weeks before the parade and could not take part, but he and his wife Alison came with my wife, Wendy, to watch the parade, and my son, Joe—unbeknownst to me—had been given special leave from school to attend the parade as well. In the 9 months leading up to the RAF100 parade, I reckon I must have lost 2.5st

---

[40] Park Run is a free to enter national timed running event that takes place in parks worldwide on Saturday mornings.

(16kg), which is equivalent to 8 bags of sugar. More importantly, this weight loss combined with my increased fitness level put my Type-2 diabetes firmly into remission.

Wendy died in November 2018, and at the start of 2019, I resolved to put my newfound fitness to work in sponsored runs for Cancer Research UK, Macmillan Cancer Support and Marie Curie. I was in the café queue with some Band on the Run mates after a park run one Saturday morning lamenting my lack of preparedness for long-distance running events and happened to be standing in front of the head coach of the BRJ Run and Tri Club, Huntingdon. He overheard my frustrations and invited me to join the club and come to the coached track sessions every Wednesday night, which I duly accepted.

The coaching staff at BRJ were and are superb and it did not take long before I was able to compete in half-marathons, and through my running, I have managed to raise a large amount of money for various cancer charities. Last year, BRJ chose Cancer Research UK as its club charity and raised £2,400 in the year I climbed Kilimanjaro. This is why I was keen to show my BRJ colours on the mountain to acknowledge how proud I am to be part of this excellent club. Moreover, I was an established BRJ member when Karen joined.

Tony, meanwhile, joined his local running club too and he has since run the London Marathon and a whole host of other long-distance events. I often tell him that his inviting me to join Band on the Run changed my life and, given how badly exposed I was to Type-2 diabetes, he probably saved my life too. He is far too humble to concur this assertion and I concede that I may have found park run under my own steam, but I will always be grateful to Tony nevertheless.

So, given my proven level of fitness, why did I struggle so much on Day 5 and why was I so exhausted? According to Peakplanet.com, approximately 1 in 3 climbers fail to reach the summit and Kilimanjaro has bested some of the world's most renowned professional athletes such as tennis legend Martina Navratilova. I considered that climbing Kilimanjaro would be difficult owing to the physical endurance required and Peakplanet.com concurs that physical preparedness is a crucial component for conquering the mountain; however, it suggests that this not the most likely reason why an individual would fail to reach the summit.

Acute Mountain Sickness (AMS) is the true enemy of success, and this is owing to the lack of oxygen at high altitude. The symptoms comprise fatigue, headache, dizziness, shortness of breath, nausea, and loss of appetite—most of which I record as experiencing in my journal. On Day 5, we were heading towards an altitude of 3,995m, which qualifies as 'Very High' in AMS terms and it is no surprise that we were all experiencing symptoms to various degrees—even Karl Mitchell, the Ironman on our team.

The main strategy for combating AMS is to take everything slowly—*Pole-Pole*—and to allow the body to naturally acclimatise to the lack of oxygen at higher altitudes; nevertheless, *Pole-Pole* does not guarantee that climbers will not succumb. The most dominant factor according to Peakplanet.com is genetics—some people are just inherently more susceptible to AMS than others, and no amount of positive mental attitude would make any difference.

So, there is no shame associated with failing to reach the summit; indeed, AMS was simply another hardship that we would all have to endure that would make our conquering the summit all the more satisfying and memorable.

# Day 6: Sunday 16 October 2022

Today has been uneventful so far. We were roused at 0700, and I was already awake from probably the best night's sleep I had experienced on the mountain so far. No further health issues and I am feeling really good. The problem is that I have probably blocked my system now with the anti-diarrhoea tablets and I have not been able to produce—I hope that this does not cause me further problems.

*Climbers were normally bunched up at the start of each day.*

We had a steep climb out of the camp and then a steady climb to another steep bit that came about at Barafu Camp. This is the base camp for the assault on the summit and it was on a steeper slope than the one we experienced yesterday; scarily, it was treacherous to walk around. We stopped to have a photo taken and then carried on. It was another steep climb, the climb that we would do later as the first part of the final ascent to Stella Point on the rim of the extinct volcano. It was tough. The plan now is to leave here at midnight, and trek/climb for another 6 hours to reach Uhuru Peak, the top, before daybreak. We will have to do the steep climb out of base camp under torchlight, so it is probably a good job that we've already had a go at the route.

We had lunch at about 1300 and afterwards the dream team of 11 guides joined us for the final brief. Each one of them gave us a bit of advice and a good luck message, and I became rather emotional. We then went to bed in the little green tents, and I managed to drift off to sleep again—I have slept so much on this trip.

I have noticed that my solar charged powerpack doesn't work and so I've decided to save however much battery life I have left on my smartphone to take some pictures at the summit. I think it is just too cold for the powerpack to perform. I am very much looking forward to descending tomorrow and reacquainting myself with the African heat. I am also looking forward to gaining the summit after what feels like a lifetime of trekking through the mountain. I am very pleased with my kit, and I haven't had to use my sleeping bag liner. I have always been toasty in the tent, but it is such a faff having to unzip everything to go to the toilet in the middle of the night.

I am excited about returning to the lodge where I just have to run the gauntlet of the mosquitoes. That has been a real treat, no mosquitoes. They do not seem to like it at this height. I have seen some house flies, but happily not many. The collared ravens are still with us, they seem to have no problems with the altitude. So, with a 2300 (11pm) muster for a midnight climb to the summit, the climbers all tried to get some sleep. I went to my bag at 1930 and fell asleep until about 2230. I just had time to dream about showing the previous owner of my house around the Willows, and then lead my friends over to the Wetherspoon's bar, and then it was time to get up. My dreams made no sense to me whatsoever!

*** 

Reflecting on this part of the journal, I am wondering why I became so emotional at the final brief. I am well known for wearing my heart on my sleeve; indeed, I sob when they hand the restored car back to the owner on the TV show, Car SOS—*they've fixed the old man's car for him!* I bawled my eyes out at the end of Toy Story 4, and as for the Muppet Christmas Carol! It made no sense to be emotional at the briefing; however, when I reflect on that particular point in the expedition, all 22 of us were there and I felt a strong connection to everyone—they were my friends.

I also felt a close bond with the brilliant guides that led us safely to this point and I listened intently to all their sagely advice.

*Some of our wonderfully cheerful and inspirational guides.*

We were only 6 hours away from conquering the summit and I believe that the emotion was owing to a niggling concern that I would not have sufficient left in the tank to make it to the top. It's not in the official list of AMS symptoms, but I think the lack of oxygen was also contributing to my hyper-emotion and my seeping tear ducts.

Reflecting on the expedition has been a journey in itself. I did not embark on the Kilimanjaro climb to find a formula for happiness, but that is certainly what it became. That night shivering in the mess tent listening carefully to the guides' advice, I knew that every single person there would do whatever they could to help me reach the summit and I would do my utmost to help them too—our mutual support did not have to be declared, it was a given. I had met most of these people only a few days before, and yet that night they were the most important people to me in the whole world.

The RAF motto is *Per Ardua Ad Astra*, which means *Through Struggle to the Stars*. I have lived with that motto since I first took an interest in the RAF as a spotty 13-year-old joining the Welwyn Garden City Air Training Corps Squadron in 1979, but over the years I stopped seeing it, I stopped thinking about what it truly meant. We were all huddled into that freezing cold, draughty mess tent hours before the final climb to Stella Point, and it was going to be an epic struggle. This is, perhaps, a metaphor for life—anything worth doing will be a struggle, learning to play an instrument, training to run a marathon, conquering Mount Kilimanjaro, finding happiness.

At the introduction, I mentioned that during my trip on the Orient Express in April of that year I read a self-help book, which *inter alia* extoled the virtues of journal writing as a means of finding happiness. I have read many such books over the years and have examined many 'formulas' for improving one's life and living happily. Most of these formulas are based on case studies of people, laymen and professionals, that have undertaken specific activities, such as journaling; have practiced mindfulness; eschewed social media and 'doom scrolling'; and a whole host of other activities that contribute to a happy life. I have tried many such suggestions with varying degrees of success.

The outcome of the Kilimanjaro expedition clearly points me towards connecting with people; I am happy when I am connected to like-minded and inspirational people, and I have no future as a loner or recluse. But herein lies the rub, I don't believe that there can be a one-size-fits-all formulaic approach to finding happiness. What works for one person cannot necessarily be rolled out as best practice—some people are happy doom scrolling social media, for example.

The last line of the poem *Desiderata* states simply *Strive to be happy*. I have never truly appreciated this simple maxim. To strive is defined in the Concise Oxford Dictionary as: *make great efforts to achieve or obtain something.*

*Desiderata* sets out some excellent advice to navigate a path through life but entreats us to make great efforts to achieve happiness. In other words, happiness doesn't just happen, it requires hard work to succeed, just like everything else. Reflecting on my trip to Kilimanjaro has taught me to look again more closely at the things that make me happy and to understand why they make me happy. It follows that if I understand what makes me happy, I can do more off it.

The converse must also be true; reflecting on the things that make you unhappy means you can try to avoid such things in the future. Was I tearful at the brief because I was unhappy? Unhappy at the thought of letting my friends down, unhappy at potentially failing to conquer the summit? I don't think any of these are true. As much as I try, I cannot understand why I was tearful at the final briefing, which goes to prove that reflective practice is not easy either. I'll put it down to a symptom of AMS and leave it at that.

# Day 7: Monday 17 October 2002 (D-Day)

We mustered at 2355 to have a last bowl of porridge and we were all kitted out for the climb to begin at midnight. I had two pairs of socks on, long johns, base layer, tee-shirt, fleece, hiking trousers and my Mammut jacket. I decided not to wear my balaclava, but I did don my Nepalese hat. I had the thin gloves on to start with and later I put my ski gloves on over the top. We were climbing by torch light and the strap on mine had broken about an hour before setting off. Thank goodness I brought a sewing kit (I had already had to repair my gloves earlier in the trip).

I worried about overheating even though the temperature was expected to fall to -20 degrees. The climb to the summit was 1200m and it was steep. I figured that I would generate enough heat of my own lifting my 90kg body that high, and I was proved right (I weighed in at 90kg at the ranger station before we started the climb; it is worth mentioning, however, that I was fully clothed with my boots on when I stood on the scales). The climb itself was a complete nightmare and proved to be one of the toughest challenges I have ever faced in my life—and I have done some lairy things in my time. It would take us 6 hours to reach Stella Point and we were using headtorches to illuminate the heels of the person in front. We were not the only group climbing that evening and it was really disconcerting to see the trail of headtorches seemingly disappearing into the sky—we soon learned to stop looking up.

The drill was *pole-pole*, or slowly in English, and we did not stop much in case we cooled down. I felt the cold in my hands, but the rest of me was fine. As we climbed higher the temperature dropped further and the water in my camelback froze. Luckily, I had filled my water bottle and had packed it in my rucksack inside a sock, and I had taken the added precaution of turning the bottle upside down so that it would freeze from the bottom. It still froze, but enough of the water stayed liquid to keep me hydrated. It was impossible to drink and climb, so we had a few micro-stops and took the opportunity to snack.

After 3 hours, I was convinced that I would not be able to make the climb. My hands became colder and colder, and I had developed a headache. I had not suffered much from altitude sickness owing to my garlic tablet regime, but I had never been this high—I began to get nervous. It turned out the headache was owing to the crude repair to my headtorch strap digging into my forehead. I was mightily relieved to remove the headtorch after sunrise, but that still seemed a long way off at the time; another 3 hours to be exact.

In the meantime, it was one foot in front of the other, *pole-pole*. I started to suffer breathlessness as the air became thinner and thinner, and the more altitude I gained, the more breathless I became, and it proved impossible to exert yourself. Every time you had to step up onto a large rock in front of you it was necessary to pause to restore your

114

breathing. There were many large rocks to have to step up onto and you were instantly exhausted and had to pant. Sometimes the trekker behind would bang into you, and often I would bang into the trekker in front when they suddenly stopped—we were that close to each other.

I had to dig deep and keep telling myself that I could do this—maintaining the maximum positive mental attitude. Indeed, I tried to match my cadence to a tune I was playing in my head. I don't know what it was called, but it was one of the tracks from the film *Zulu* with Michael Caine[41]. Everyone struggled with the climb, it was like nothing many of us had ever experienced.

I am writing up this journal tucked up in my sleeping bag with my headtorch donned for light. I feel like Captain Scott again. I did not expect to feel so cold—it's Africa, for goodness' sake. It makes a lie of the classic line from the Band Aid single: *There won't be snow in Africa this Christmas time…* I am so looking forward to descending the last 3000m tomorrow and being warm again. I am really looking forward to getting back to the lodge and having a good shower, and maybe getting some of my kit laundered for the trip home to Blighty. All my kit is *minging*, as the Scots would say, and I have been washing in a small bowl for the last 7 days.

---

[41] When I returned from Kilimanjaro, I realized that the tune I had in my head was the *Main Theme from Zulu* written by John Barry. Listening to the *Main Theme from Zulu* on YouTube, for example, would give readers a good idea of the climbing cadence. For the musicians, I'd say it was between 'Lento' and 'Larghetto', 50–60 beats per minute. You don't just learn to play an instrument at music school.

Back to the climb, we stopped for a quick drink and a snack, and the guide reported that there was only 30 minutes remaining until we reached Stella Point, which is on the old crater rim. We were briefed that it was another 40 minutes gentle climb to Uhuru Peak from this point.

*Sunrise at the top of Mount Kilimanjaro.*

Well, 30 minutes passed or thereabouts and we arrived at Stella Point at around 0600. There were many emotional people on that rim that had all suffered the same doubts and with manifold medical and physiological issues. Jennie and I had a little cry and a hug. The view from Stella Point was already spectacular—the sky was still full of stars, but it was starting to get lighter, and presently a big orange band appeared on the horizon. Steadily, the orange band became thicker and brighter until the sun finally appeared in all its divine glory—we could feel the first rays of warmth on our cold and tired cheeks. Headtorches were unceremoniously removed and stowed, and we trekked for a further 40 minutes on a gentle slope to reach the summit. I have seldom seen anything so beautiful.

*The Author resting at the top of Mount Kilimanjaro after one of the most grueling but exhilarating experiences of his life.*

When we arrived at Uhuru Peak, the sun was a big red ball in the sky and it was being reflected on the cloud base, so there were effectively 2 suns—the ultimate reflection! It was then that we were able to fully appreciate the scenery. The top of Kilimanjaro is a crater, it is a dormant volcano, and it is topped by spectacular glaciers. There are other secondary peaks[42] that poke up majestically above the cloud blanket—it was a truly awesome spectacle that no photograph could ever do justice to; you had to be there, and we were there—and I found myself overwhelmed with emotion.

*Jennie Cochrane standing proudly on the Roof of Africa.*

---

[42] I believe that these were Kibo and Mawenzi.

We all gathered around the signpost at the summit and more tears were shed. It was appropriate to remember the people that we had lost, and Jim unfurled a picture of his brother Andrew, and I unpacked my small England flag to remember Wendy. I had one of the cancer care brooches she used to wear in my pack having nearly lost it on the trek, and I did consider leaving it at the summit. I brought it back down with me to return it to the treasure box I keep in the loft with all the things that were important to her.

Owing to all the emotion and sheer joy of reaching the summit, I did not initially register that 5 members of our party were missing. We were only allowed 15–20 minutes at the top to minimise altitude sickness, which I had not suffered from. So, we made our way back to Stella Point. We paused to prepare our kit for the descent when 4 of our missing companions appeared. They were being led by a guide called 'Moses', rather apt I thought, and the other guides were 'singing them in', calling out the names of the trekkers and waving their arms in the air. It was a lovely sight to see and very well received.

We left the happy 4 to head up to the summit and then made the final preparations for the descent. There was still a trekker missing, however. It was Toby, and he had really struggled throughout the climb. We descended on the scree slope and as we did so, we saw that Toby was still at least 20 minutes from Stella Point—but he was still going! We gave him a rousing cheer as we attacked the scree. This was much more rapid than the climb and we found ourselves sliding (skiing) on the scree, which took us to the bottom of the slope in about an hour.

It took only a further 2 hours to reach basecamp, and with 30 minutes to go my porter, Richard, appeared and met me on the trail. He took my rucksack from me and carried it the rest of the way and we arrived back at basecamp at 0900; so, we had been 9 hours on the trail. Richard seemed really pleased to see me and was all smiles and joy as we trekked back together—he is such a top bloke.

We rested for a short while and then had another 3-hour trek to Millenium Camp—our final camp on the trip. It was a fairly easy trek compared to that of the night before, and I walked along chatting happily to Jennie. Karen had urged me to use the trip to rebuild bridges with Wendy's family and I think I did just that—*Wendy's family is my family*. Jennie and I spoke about many things, and I am confident that all is mended between us—I very much hope so.

We arrived at the camp before the porters, which was not normal, and we watched them pitch the tents. It was a well-drilled routine and our campsite literally appeared in front of us in minutes. Before we set off, the 4 trekkers that had arrived late at Stella Point appeared in the camp, but there was no sign of Toby. Everyone that arrived at the last camp was totally exhausted—we had been trekking for 12 hours. So, we all lazed about in the tents, and when tea was called at 1700, only 4 of us pitched up at the mess tent. Dinner was at 1830, and happily Toby arrived in camp just before—he had been trekking for 18 hours, and sadly he did not make the summit. He made it to Stella Point, and we all felt very sorry for him, but he was in really good form; indeed, the grit and determination he had shown to reach Stella Point was inspirational.

I had no appetite and did not eat much. Then I became very cold waiting for the chief guide, Tony Blair, to give us the brief for the morning. There are no roads in the park, so we had a 13km hike to the transport to look forward to in the morning. So, it was to be another 0600 reveille and we must be on the trek for 0730, which would ensure that we arrived at the park gate and transport hub at 1230. Tony Blair informed us that there would be a buffet lunch waiting for us so we could eat before boarding the transport to take us back to the lodge, which was a 2-hour drive away.

So, the mountain is climbed and the bridges built—mission accomplished. How do I feel? Exhausted, but in a really good way. I have not enjoyed being disconnected from Karen and my family, and I have really missed my home comforts. That said, disconnecting from Facebook has been really good for me and I am resolved to spend less time browsing Facebook videos when I return home. I had heard only snippets of news, but again I had learned to live without it.

I have also been 'dry'—there was no alcohol in the park, and I have coped okay without it. In short, I am feeling good. So, I am going to curb my alcohol consumption henceforth and I am going to sign up to run a marathon next year to give some focus to my training. Would I come to Kilimanjaro again? Not on your life!

\*\*\*

*Per Ardua ad Astra*, the RAF motto that translates to 'through struggle to the stars', seems wholly appropriate to describe that final climb. The struggle was epic, and the destination was Stella Point, or 'star' point, which was aptly named. All credit to the guides that brought us to Stella Point immediately before the dawn, it was the most amazing experience to watch the sunrise from there, and I well remember the huge orange band, that was actually curved, appearing in the sky to the east of the mountain moments before we saw the sun. I also remember feeling somewhat overwhelmed with emotion; I was bursting with pride at the huge sense of achievement against some of the toughest challenges I had ever faced.

It is astonishing that 21 out of the 22 climbers made it to Uhuru Peak against an expected 1 in 3 failure rate. Moreover, Toby, through dogged determination and bloody-mindedness, made it to Stella Point, and I am certain that he would have made it to the summit had there been more time. I was only sorry that he reached Stella Point on his own because from my perspective, the fact that I reached the summit with so many of my mates is what made the experience all the more pleasurable and memorable. Indeed, when I reflect on that moment in time, I realised that this is what had been missing from my life—mutual endeavour and achievement.

When Wendy died, I withdrew from all the activities that brought me into contact with other people. I did not appreciate that engaging with my students as their tutor was a form of mutual endeavour, and when they achieved their degrees and/or professional recognition, the achievement was mutual. Moreover, I did not appreciate that playing an instrument in a band was also a form of mutual endeavour, and the standing ovation received at the end of the concert, the epitome of mutual achievement.

Suddenly, all the months of practice to master my musical instrument made sense. Being able to play an instrument does not necessarily mean that you will be able to play as part of a band; it takes practice, it is often a struggle, there are many errors made and setbacks that have to be corrected over many weeks, even months. But when it all comes together and the audience applauds loudly, the weeks of sore lips and blistered fingers suddenly prove worthwhile. Indeed, these hardships amplify the enjoyment of the achievement. Park Run on Saturday mornings is another form of mutual endeavour that I now view in a different light. I keep going every Saturday morning because it makes me happy, and it is something that I do with my friends.

When I wear my running club colours on the slopes of Mount Kilimanjaro or when taking part in an organised running event, I am connected to a group of like-minded people, that also appreciate being connected to me. I am happy when I am connected to other human beings, and nothing connects me better to other human beings than mutual endeavour and achievement—who knew? So, the last line of my journal entry, 'not on your life!' should probably be cast into oblivion.

I probably did not make a conscious decision to withdraw from the activities that made me happy after Wendy died, but another thing to consider is that everyone was compelled to withdraw from human contact early in 2020. As the inquiry into the handling of the Covid-19 pandemic gets underway in earnest there are increasing daily reports of a growing mental health crisis, especially amongst the younger members of society. As children, we would all probably have welcomed the schools closing for protracted periods not realising that the hardship and toil associated with lessons is accompanied by the joy of socialising with friends.

Children missed out on the mutual endeavour of team sports and after school clubs, etc, where their connections to other like-minded children were irredeemably severed. It does not take a leap of faith to link the isolation of lockdown with the seeming deterioration in the mental health not only of our children, but also in the adult population. It is particularly sad, however, that our children are continuing to suffer on account of industrial action and all parties owe it to our children to resolve these issues as soon as possible.

I would like to think that making and maintaining connections with other human beings is easy, but of course this is not the case. Reaching out to other people is not without risk, and this is particularly acute in affairs of the heart. Breaking up with a lover, spouse, partner, or sole mate can be devastating and I know several family members and friends that dare not expose themselves to such heartbreak again. Indeed, I have been tempted to eschew relationships forever after experiencing heartbreak and I appreciate that reaching out again requires courage.

At the height of the pandemic, I was taken with the poem that appears at the end of the brilliant 2019 film *JoJo Rabbit*, which is set during the Second World War and focuses on the Nazi terror inflicted on the Jews. I have been thinking about this poem again in the light of further conflict between Israel and Hamas in the Gaza Strip recently. *JoJo Rabbit* is both heartbreaking and uplifting, and the quote at the end reads:

*Let everything happen to you.*
*Beauty and terror.*

*Just keep going.*
*No feeling is final.*

The quote is from the 'Book of Hours' written by Rainer Maria Rilke, a German poet. I have this poem framed in my study and when I have been particularly sad or heartbroken, it is comforting to consider that I won't feel this way forever. I found this idiom invaluable on Mount Kilimanjaro—*just keep going*. We made it to Uhuru Peak because we just kept going, Toby made it to Stella Point because he just kept going. We succeed in life when we all just keep going, and that is a huge source of comfort. The maxim cuts both ways, unfortunately; happiness is not final either!

Nevertheless, Rilke inspires me to think that if I fail or end up heartbroken again, there will always be new happiness to look forward to. Feelings associated with heartbreak are very difficult to dismiss as not being final, but I know from experience that if you do have the courage to reach out again then new happiness awaits. Karen joined my running club at a time when my life appeared to be at rock bottom. Like me, Karen had suffered immeasurable heartbreak and yet she just kept going and the upshot is that together we have found new happiness.

So, when I reflect on my trip to Kilimanjaro, I do so with immense fondness—it was a hugely happy time. In writing up my journal and analysing why I felt the way I did or behaved the way I did, I have found a new philosophy for living happily, and I intend to be happy.

# Last Day on the Mountain: Tuesday 18 October 2022

I woke up at 0530 after the worst night's sleep I had experienced on the mountain. I was nice and warm, but the tent was pitched on a slope, and I kept sliding down to the bottom—not great! It is a frosty morning, and the inside of the tent is covered in ice. I am so fed up being cold, but after a 13k hike today, we should be in the sunny African heat. It looks like we will not be back at the hotel until 4pm this afternoon. That's okay as long as I don't have to spend another night in this tiny tent.

The porter had just brought me a mug of black tea. I seem to have acquired a taste for black tea. There has been no fresh milk on the expedition, and we must use creamer in lieu. I tried my tea with creamer and then tried it without, and without tastes better. I forgot to mention that I had a gushing nosebleed this morning—thank goodness for wet wipes.

It is now 0615 and the sun is just showing itself behind a ridge to the east of the camp. I know that as soon as it crests the ridge the sun will bathe the camp in a warm glow, and I will be able to strip down for *washy-washy*—hopefully for the last time.

It is now 0630 and the *washy-washy* water has arrived, but the sun has yet to crest the ridge. It is unbelievable the difference the sun makes. As I look out of the tent, all the other tents are covered in frost—it does not encourage stripping off to wash. I did not have to wait much longer and when the sun did breach the ridge, the camp was transformed. Presently, the male campers stripped off and began to wash themselves down. It is amazing how clean you can make yourself with a small amount of water—perhaps a good lesson to consider given the shortages of water we experienced in Cambridgeshire last summer.

After *washy-washy*, I went to the mess tent for breakfast and the camp was buzzing with the excitement of heading down the mountain. As usual, my kit was already packed and after a quick toothbrush and a final prep, I was ready to go. I set off with the lead crew and at the start we walked on what appeared to be a prepared track. I say prepared, but it was still very rough, and you had to watch your footing. Soon though, the path became smoother, but the slope was still very gentle, and the going was easy—only 13km to go. It was predicted to take 5 hours, but we convinced ourselves that we could do it faster.

What we did not expect was how steep and hazardous the trail would become. Nevertheless, we soldiered on and were making good time. I could tell through the pain in my knees that we were descending, and the scenery was becoming less and less barren. Indeed, the path eventually led into a rain forest but before we entered the forest we came to another camp and took the opportunity to regroup and *mark our territory* for those that needed to—me included.

I set off from the new camp with Annabel (Bel), Jennie (sister-in-law) and Roddy. At this point, our porters began to overtake us, so we were constantly moving to one side of the path to let them pass and calling 'Jambo' to say hello. The porters are an amazing bunch of people. They were each carrying at least 30kg plus their own kit, and they easily outpaced us. They also seemed much more sure-footed and there were many of them—there were at least two groups of trekkers descending the mountain that day and we had 75 porters supporting our party alone. So, there was nearly a constant stream of porters passing by.

We were now totally in the rainforest and it was becoming quite misty. The more we descended, the more we heard birdsong, and some rather exotic-looking birds flew above us in the trees. We also saw monkeys and remarked that only a week ago we would have all become overexcited to see them and would have been reaching for the cameras, but they somehow seemed old hat to us now.

*I'm writing up my journal sat outside my lodge at 1150 on Wednesday morning, and there is a family of small monkeys staring down at me from one of the nearby trees. They are very quiet, but I can hear other monkeys chirping away in the near distance.*

I walked behind Jennie and Bel, and they were telling each other their life stories. It was good for me because Jennie related her whole career and explained to Bel how her life chances came about and why she chose various paths. I have known Jennie for over 25 years, and I was largely ignorant of her life and career. What an opportunity, and I reflected upon how many other people would be given the opportunity to get to know their in-laws so well.

The trek continued and the path became steeper and the atmosphere more humid, so I delayered my clothing and removed my gaiters. I also removed my hat and tucked it into my rucksack belt, and I stowed my sunglasses. We were shaded under the rainforest canopy, so I was not worried about sunburn. Indeed, I could tell we were getting lower because we were getting warmer—finally!

Still the porters filed past us, and we continued to shout *Jambo* to all of them; sometimes fist-bumping them as well. I quipped to my companions that I would be likely to greet everyone in Huntingdon High Street the same way next week. We continued down the mountain along the jungle path, which continued to get steeper and more rugged. Our small band of trekkers began to peel off the path to *ease springs*, and I had to do the same several times. It was a bit disconcerting leaving the path to step into the jungle for a pee—I was fearful of coming face to face with an apex predator! Suddenly, I found myself alone in the thickening rainforest—a totally weird sensation, and I had a mischievous thought about hiding in the bushes and jumping out on Jennie when she eventually caught up with me. I figured, however, that it would be difficult to complete the remainder of the trek with a walking pole shoved up my backside.

There was still a long way to go when I had another nosebleed. I had no option but to plug my nostril with a tissue and press on. This raised some funny looks from the porters, but it did the job. On and on, we hiked until eventually we reached a checkpoint where we saw our first vehicle. It was a white 4x4 jeep kitted out as an ambulance. I rejoiced at the fact that the appearance of the ambulance meant that the remainder of the trek to the gate would be on a road of sorts, at least the sort of road a 4x4 could navigate.

After another short regroup, we descended along the road with about another hour left to march. By this time, my knees were on fire. Having watched a huge number of porters speed past us on the trail with no incidents, one of them eventually lost his footing and fell over, spilling his load onto the road. Before we could get to him to offer our assistance, he had dusted himself off, remounted his load and was on his way again. He showed us how remarkably robust and resilient these people could be.

At long last, we saw the roof of the gatehouse at the end of the trail—our trek was at an end. Hallelujah! There was a relatively normal washroom and restaurant at the gatehouse, and we all took advantage—they had porcelain! There was a small kiosk outside selling bottles of coke and beers, and we took advantage of that as well. A couple of guys approached us while we were waiting for the rest of the party and offered to clean out boots for $2. All of us took up the offer and before long all our boots were gleaming—relatively speaking. I enjoyed a bottle of Kilimanjaro lager and together with my expedition buddies we toasted our achievement.

Eventually, there we 21 trekkers present at the gate—the 22nd team member was Toby and there was no sign of him. We knew that the guides would not leave him, but we were concerned about him nevertheless. After a short while, the 4x4 ambulance that we had seen parked at the end of the jungle path appeared and a smiling Toby emerged from the back of it. He was not injured, thankfully, but he had been with 'Tony Blair' the chief guide and Tony had some things prepared for us and did not want Toby holding up proceedings. So, Toby had been urged politely to cadge a lift in the back of the ambulance.

We welcomed Toby into the fold and plied him with lager. We had his boots cleaned for him and settled into a round of photo-taking to mark the occasion of everyone arriving back from Kilimanjaro safely. The chefs from the expedition had made it down much earlier, and they had prepared a brilliant buffet lunch for us. This was laid out in the gatehouse restaurant, and it comprised a range of delicious African fayre. We were in for a real treat after the meal. The porters and guides were lined up outside the restaurant and they sung one of their traditional African songs for us at the 'Tipping' ceremony.

David Cochrane (Big D) was in charge of awarding the tips and he started with the ordinary porters (nothing ordinary about these people). The erstwhile trekkers were all stood in a line and the porters filed passed us for a fist bump and a thank-you. Then Dave awarded the main porters their tip and they duly filled passed the line of trekkers to receive their fist-bumps and thank-you messages.

When Richard, my personal porter, passed me, I stopped him and made a gift of my mum's scarf. He gave me his usual beaming smile and a huge hug. He was absolutely delighted, and I was overwhelmed at how such a small gesture could have such a huge effect. I did not even consider how I would explain my actions to my mum! She had knitted the scarf especially for my trip, but I somehow knew she would be delighted too.

The rest of the tips were given out and we were treated to more renditions of African singing—it was complete unadulterated joy. One guy stands in front of the porters and chants a phrase, which receives a mighty response from them all. Their voices were shrill but tuneful and you could feel the energy in the air around you. The singing was so wonderful, so extraordinary that I became overwhelmed with emotion. My vision blurred as my eyes filled with tears of joy and as I looked around, I could see that most of my companions were experiencing the same thing. King James, one of the senior guides, then took to the front of the crowd and led another song, and the porters and guides started dancing.

Despite the manifold-tired legs and aching knees, all the trekkers joined in with them and there were beaming smiles everywhere. I will never ever forget that experience. Wonderful! It was quite simply one of the most joyous experiences of my life—second only, perhaps, to the birth of my son. Joy! Joy! Joy! It was the most beautiful way to end the trek and say goodbye to the people we had come to know (and love) so well.

Eventually, our porters and guides marched away with more fist-bumps and hugs, and then we boarded the buses for the 2-hour-long journey back to the lodge. The road immediately beyond the gate brought the Tanzanian poverty rapidly back into focus. The road out of the park was lined with shanty cabins with miserable looking women sat on buckets or crates waiting for customers to purchase their scanty wares. There were many scrawny goats nibbling at the verges and it did not look like there was any grass on these verges to nourish them. These goats were normally being looked after by children, some of whom looked to be only 5 or 6 years of age.

As we travelled on, we passed a huge coffee plantation and saw many women harvesting the beans, some with babies swaddled on their backs. As our journey progressed, there seemed to be no end to the rows and rows of austere shops and stalls lining the road. Some appeared very rundown but had modern signs above them such as Vodafone, and we saw banks and cash machines amongst the shanty shops. There were also some weird combinations, one shop said: *Nancy's Cake and Tools*. Now there's something Screwfix had not thought of back home: "Could I have a set of Allen Keys, a 2lb lump hammer and a slice of Victoria sponge please?"

There were also a good number of coffin shops with some of the most gawdy coffins I have ever seen on display outside. I nearly wrote *on the forecourt* then, but none of the shops had anything resembling a forecourt, only a flattened area of the orange Tanzanian mud. One shop had an even more gawdy hearse parked outside, which was decorated all over in black and gold, looking like something straight out of the *Addams Family*.

The bus continued its journey back to the lodge and the roadside towns became busier. We passed some schools with children out playing in dusty, orange-tinged fields. I was amazed to see huge termite mounds on the school fields and reflected on the fact that I get upset when an ants' nest appears in my lawn. The Tanzanians seem to have learned to live with the termites. Later in the trip we saw the children walking home from school; some tiny, but all of them walking home unaccompanied. Some were walking through the dodgiest looking neighbourhoods. They all appeared to be very smart, that said—decent shoes, ties and jumpers. Some were obviously Muslim children with their heads and legs covered—the girls that is. Indeed, this morning at the lodge, we heard the call to prayer.

As we moved out of Moshi, we encountered a hold-up and found ourselves in a huge cloud of dust. A large lorry carrying some sort of screed had overturned and had blocked the road, but all the other traffic was simply driving around the wreckage on to the dirt verge—hence the dust cloud. Our bus negotiated the crash site and continued on. Although I was exhausted, I found the sights fascinating and did not want to miss out.

Eventually, we came to the road that led up to the lodge— I say road, it was more of a dust track. As the bus progressed towards the lodge, the standard of buildings dropped again, and the people looked miserable again. Some children waved at us, and some of the young girls were very well presented with their hair braided and covered in beads. As we drove further up the track, which was no more that the width of the bus, motorcycles passed either side of us, all of them with pillion passengers. These were most probably the taxis.

Eventually, our bus came face to face with a large 4x4 jeep, and our driver had to reverse the bus back down the track to let the jeep into a side road—the bus was lurching frighteningly from side to side as it reversed and, for a moment, I thought we were going to slide off into the ditch.

Our driver pressed on to the lodge and came to a halt on the paved drive opposite reception. We wasted no time disembarking and we quickly signed in at reception, dumped our kit, and then proceeded with all haste to the bar. After a few swift beers, I went back to the basher[43] to shower, and it was the best shower I had experienced since before the trek. So nice to be able to stand up at a sink as well.

I was astonished by my appearance; I hadn't been near a mirror or a razor for so long, and I looked like Grizzly Adams[44]. There was nothing I could do as I had not brought any shaving kit, so the beard would have to stay until I arrived home. I am not keeping the beard; it was too white and made me look so much older. So, all nice and clean, I returned to the bar for dinner.

Dinner was brilliant. It was a mixed buffet and I enjoyed it very much after expedition rations. After dinner, the party started and we all congregated around the firepit. I should also mention that after dinner we stayed at the table and a few of the trekkers delivered some very emotional speeches as the completion certificates were handed out. Jim Fairlie became very emotional, and he set everyone else off. I am very proud of my certificate. But I'm not sure how to pack the certificate to avoid damaging it. I'm sure I'll be able to flatten it out once I get home.

*I have just received the call to board the bus for the terminal.*

---

[43] '*Basher*' is another nod to my military associations and was the name used for the lodgings when I stayed at Ascension Island in 1992.

[44] Grizzly Adams was a popular children's programme in the 1980s where the main character was an aging hirsute gentleman that lived wild in North America with a grizzly bear as a pet.

We have arrived at the airport (it is 1750 Tanzanian time and I have just made it through security, and I'm now waiting to check in).

The journey to the airport was just over an hour and we took in the usual scenes of Tanzanian life—I never seem to tire watching the locals go about their business.

***

There are many sights from my trip to Africa that I will never forget, and most of these are not what many people would expect. I was in awe of the lions, elephants, gorgeous sunsets, jaw-dropping mountain vistas, etc; but it was the seemingly innocuous everyday sights that had the most profound effect on me. One such sight was the schoolboys in their smart school uniforms that I saw disembarking from the yellow people carrier, which stopped in front of our crew bus on the dusty orange track that led to the lodge we stayed at before the climb. They waved to us with beaming smiles as they made their merry way into the forest, and I wondered what sort of home they could be heading back to amongst the trees.

We saw many groups of children walking home from school on our travels and it was hugely encouraging to also see young girls amongst these groups. Indeed, I observed Muslim girls walking home from school, many of whom were wearing hijabs colour-coordinated with their school uniforms, and this too was deeply reassuring. I had been loosely following the plight of the women in Afghanistan adjusting to Taliban rule after more than 20 years of direct western involvement. I hoped that the outlook for Muslim girls in Tanzania was much brighter.

Since I returned from Africa in October 2022, there has been a constant drip feed of news from Afghanistan relating to the rapid foreshortening of opportunities for women. Initially, the Taliban pledged to follow a more liberal line to allow women to work and be educated; however, these rights have been steadily eroded since the Taliban returned to power in 2021. A news item from the BBC website in March 2023 reads:

*Afghan universities have begun reopening after a winter break, but the new term is another painful reminder to young women of how their world is shrinking.*

The article paints a very gloomy picture and there were statements from women that had been studying for degrees and even PhDs who were now being excluded from completing those studies. The BBC article reports that the Taliban's treatment of women and girls has outraged the international community and has increased Afghanistan's isolation at a time when its economy is collapsing. The BBC article also states that a recent UN report implied that the restrictions on women could amount to crimes against humanity. I doubt very much whether the UN report would cause the Taliban any consternation after the west, particularly USA, lost patience with the Afghan intervention.

I am not sufficiently well versed in the Quran scripts to assert whether the subjugation of women is truly part of Islamic doctrine; I am more inclined to think that the Taliban is fearful of empowering women through work and education.

Empowered women might pose too great a threat to the Taliban's patriarchal culture.

In my second career as an associate lecturer for the Open University, I had seen first-hand the empowerment education can deliver and how it can change people's lives for the better. In 2015, I was supervising an engineering master's student on her team design project, which was the final module she had to complete to earn her Master of Science (MSc) degree. She had been in part-time education for nearly 17 years and her story was inspirational.

My student had been serving as a junior rank in the RAF when she became pregnant. Unfortunately, her daughter was born with profound disabilities and her husband quit the relationship, which compelled my student to leave the RAF to care for her daughter as a single parent. Initially, she worked as an unqualified assistant at the school her daughter attended, until she decided that she had to do something to better provide for them.

17 years earlier, she had enrolled on an engineering foundation course—she had no previous experience of engineering or commensurate qualifications, but she found the subject matter appealing. She devoted her spare time to study for nearly a decade to eventually be admitted to the Open University Degree of Bachelor of Science in Mechanical Engineering. But she *just kept going*; she then spent the next 7 years studying for an MSc, for which I was one of her last tutors.

I am proud to say that she passed with flying colours and later the Engineering Council conferred her the title of chartered engineer. This is a wonderful story, but as her skills, knowledge and experience grew so did her standing in industry. Initially, she secured employment in a junior technical role within a specialist manufacturing company, and as her studies ensued, she continued to earn promotions and widen her span of control and influence. Just before she secured her MSc, she became a director at an international engineering corporation. Her daughter, now in her early 20s, had been provided with all the support she needed growing up, and my student had re-married; her future and that of her family was incredibly bright. There were many such stories punctuating my 15 years in academia, and thus I continue to advocate education as a key enabler in personal and, indeed, global development.

I was excited therefore to see how the Tanzanian government was making education available to all—even setting up schools in the middle of the Ngorongoro plain for the Massai children tending their goats. I wondered at how far the children could go, did they have technical colleges and universities? This question was answered for me recently when I had to undergo physiotherapy to recover from a running injury. My physiotherapist spotted the Kilimanjaro logo on the back of my jacket and reported happily that he was from Arusha. He had been in England for 5 years and he informed me that Tanzania had a world-class selection of universities, including specialist universities for agriculture, science and technology, engineering and, of course, healthcare. The degrees obtained from these universities were accredited worldwide, and he told me that most of the students he studied with had left Tanzania soon after completing their degrees, many of them heading for Europe.

My physiotherapist put a simple question to me; if you could earn 3–4 times your potential Tanzanian earnings and live in a prosperous country such as the UK, would you stay in Arusha? I had never really considered that by encouraging medical professionals to come to the UK to work in the NHS we were potentially depriving developing countries of the people they had invested in. So instead of being a global development enabler, education in developing nations could be viewed as a means for the best and brightest to quit their country. How does the international community balance this conundrum? There are no easy answers, but ultimately the risk of losing the best and brightest abroad should not preclude educating people in the first place.

The BBC article[45] on the barring of women from universities in Afghanistan included a statement from a former student:

*My plan was to finish university, do my masters, and then my PhD. I wanted to work and serve my nation, my people, my country. I can't do that now.*

Maybe this sentiment is a reason for optimism, maybe a larger proportion of the doctors, nurses, engineers, etc that Tanzania educates will remain and help the county to develop—what might the Tanzanian government do to encourage them to stay? I also wonder whether European nations, especially the UK, might also have a moral obligation to reduce their reliance on key workers from developing nations; perhaps European nations should invest more in training and educating their own citizens.

---

[45] Ibid

Tony Blair—the real one, not our Kilimanjaro guide—during his tenure as leader of the opposition, famously stated that the Labour Party's priorities in government were Education, Education, Education. This doctrine was manifest in a government target to send 50% of school leavers to university, and at the time this appeared to be a sensible policy to adapt the UK workforce to the 'post-industrial era', where the prevailing trend was for major manufacturing to be off shored. The government of the day postulated that the UK would need more graduates, but the outcome of this policy proved catastrophic for a generation of school leavers and for the UK as a whole.

The Great University Con[46] examines the consequences of the university expansion including the huge pressure placed on school leavers to go to university whether they were likely to benefit or not, the lowering of entrance standards to fill ever-increasing numbers of courses, falling academic standards, an immense oversupply of graduates compared to available job opportunities, and—most worryingly of all—graduates burdened with unrepayable debts that eventually have to be picked up by the tax payer.

I was fortunate to be a school leaver when the country invested in its future doctors, scientists and engineers through grant-funded university places, and industry invested in its artisans and craftsmen through indentured apprenticeships and vocational training. I enrolled with British Aerospace, as it was then called, in 1984 as an apprentice electronic technician, and showed sufficient aptitude that the firm

---

[46] *The Great University Con*, Craig and Openshaw, the Original Book Company, 2018.

sponsored me to study on a degree course, which I graduated from in 1989. I had a small overdraft to pay, but nothing compared to the debt that today's graduates are saddled with.

In the 1980s, only 15%[47] of school leavers attended university and undergraduates' parents were means tested to discern a parental contribution to maintenance grants—all tuition fees were paid by the respective local authority. 30 years later, 50%[48] of school leavers attend university and the country can no longer afford to invest in them.

Potentially the most pernicious outcome, however, is the social implication that not going to university somehow makes the school leaver a second-class citizen. The Great University Con suggests that expectations of parents, teachers and peers make it difficult for any young person to choose any post-school option other than university[49]. It quotes figures published from the Times Higher Education supplement where surveys showed that 76% of undergraduates had not been informed of alternatives to university before leaving school and of these 46% would have undertaken an apprenticeship or vocational training instead. Apprenticeships and vocational training are, however, expensive and with the added influence of society effectively discouraging youngsters from such schemes, UK industry became increasingly reliant on artisans and craftsmen trained overseas.

The Hotel Industry Trust (HIT) Scotland is a rare example of industry supporting and encouraging people to acquire and

---

[47] Ibid, p.3

[48] id

[49] Ibid, p.30

develop skills through scholarships and placements—industry investing in its own artisans. David Cochrane is the chief executive of HIT Scotland and I have always been incredibly proud of the work he does. I confess, however, that I did not truly appreciate the extraordinary nature of this work until I spent so much time in the company of HIT stakeholders in Tanzania. Hundreds of young people are awarded scholarships each year to study and train 'on-the-job' at some of Scotland's most prestigious hospitality venues, such as Gleneagles. They do not have to have degrees or be academically gifted, they just need to have an aptitude for their chosen trade, a commitment and positive mental attitude towards the profession, and the drive and determination to succeed—something I witnessed in spades on Mount Kilimanjaro.

Arguably one of the most prestigious scholarships that HIT Scotland awards to aspiring artisans is the Andrew Fairlie Scholarship, which has been running since 2019. David and his team have worked hard to position the Andrew Fairlie Scholarship as the ultimate educational programme that any aspiring chef in Scotland could hope to receive. Our climb to the top of Mount Kilimanjaro not only raised the profile of this wonderful scholarship, but also it raised a significant amount of money to maintain the scholarship for future generations of budding world-class chefs. That very fact makes me enormously proud to have taken part in the trek and to have stood with Jim Fairlie when he paid tribute to his brother, Andrew, on the top of the world.

HIT Scotland might be a blueprint for other industry-based initiatives that both encourage and invest in young people to attain and develop the skills that industry needs without relying on a grossly inefficient university sector? A question worthy of further debate. As for those two little schoolboys debussing from their rickety school bus along a dirt track in Tanzania, who knows... maybe one of those 2 little lads trekking into the rainforest after school will grow up to be president and will lead their country to great things.

# Wednesday 26 October 2022

HIT Scotland's expedition to Kilimanjaro is finally over, a bit like Lizz Truss's government. The trek was a truly exceptional experience, the experience of a lifetime—the mountain was climbed, and the bridges built, so I fulfilled Karen's hopes for me. Talking of Karen, I had a lovely weekend with her, and we quickly picked up where we left off. I am very keen to keep our relationship going and I am excited to find out where it might lead.

The expedition served as a good reset and I was reminded how wonderful my life is, especially when I was sat in Norwich Cathedral watching Joe's graduation. Wendy would have been very proud of him, as indeed I was as he marched up the isle at Norwich Cathedral with his first-class honours degree in hand. As he approached me, I purposefully gave him a double thumbs-up to replicate the thumbs-up he had given me when I graduated with my master of arts degree from the UK Defence Academy, Shrivenham, when Joe was only 4 years old. I enjoyed talking with his tutors at the reception afterwards. They all commented on what a great lad he had been, and I was welling up with pride. Joe is on his way now, and I am confident that his future is bright—my work here is done.

So, what of my life? It is far from perfect, but I'm sure that with a bit of patience things will work out okay. I need to press on with my plan, and I need to sort (or allow time to sort) my father out? But all in all, things look good; especially when I compare my life to that of the Massai children I met in the Ngorongoro Crater! I was given the opportunity to reflect on my experiences from a totally unique perspective; indeed, when I looked at my life from the top of Mount Kilimanjaro—the top of the world—I really liked what I saw.

**The End** (of the journal)

# Epilogue

In the year since the HIT Scotland Mount Kilimanjaro expedition returned triumphantly from Africa, my life has changed beyond all recognition and most definitely for the better. I set out to conquer the summit with a corollary mission to reconnect with Wendy's family; in particular, Jennie and David Cochrane. I stood proudly on top of the world at Uhuru Peak after one of the most physically and mentally demanding journeys I had ever experienced.

When I reached the summit, I did so not only with Jennie and David, but also with some other extraordinary people that I would have gladly and willingly made sacrifices for. I felt an overwhelming sense of loyalty towards them, and they had all supported me at some point in the expedition—even those of them that ordinarily I would have had nothing in common with. Reflecting on that moment at the top of the world, I was foolish to ever believe that I could be happy standing alone; I know now, more than ever, that I need to belong to something and someone—I need to be connected.

Moreover, I learned that connecting and reconnecting with other humans was entirely down to me. I had to reach out to people and be accommodating to other people reaching out to me. Doing so would not be without risk and it would take courage, but the rewards would always make it worthwhile.

At the end of Day 1, my journal records a quotation from an eminent writer, Charles Handy[50]. I misquoted him in the journal, but corrected his maxim in the footnotes, which reads: 'Happiness is having something to do, something to hope for and someone to love[51].' To make sure I had remembered this quotation correctly, I retrieved my collection of his books from my home library and found it in *The Elephant and the Flea*, which was first published in 2001. Before I found the right book, I also looked for Handy's maxim in *The Empty Raincoat*; here, Handy presents a powerful alternative vision of life and work grounded in a natural sense of continuity, connection and purposeful direction.

In this book written in 1994, Handy contends that loneliness may be the real disease of the next century as people increasingly live alone, work alone, and play alone; insulated from society by [their] modem, Walkman or television[52]. Thirty years later, most people might not know what a modem or a Walkman is, but we could easily swap these terms for internet and smartphone respectively. Nevertheless, Handy's prescience is remarkable considering

---

[50] Charles Handy is an independent writer, teacher and broadcaster best known for his 'Thoughts for Today' on the BBC's Today Programme.

[51] *The Elephant and the Flea*, Charles Handy, Arrow Books (2002), p.215.

[52] *The Empty Raincoat,* Charles Handy, Arrow Books (2002 Ed), p.248.

the modern culture of working from home, our absolute dependence on smartphones and our ability to stream whatever we want to watch whenever we want to watch it to our living room televisions. These are modern factors that conspire insidiously to break our connections to our fellow human beings.

My loneliness prior to joining the HIT Scotland Mount Kilimanjaro expedition was initially the result of my own folly—quitting my job, quitting music, and estranging myself from family and friends when I had not fully come to terms with losing my wife. The forced isolation associated with the Covid-19 pandemic, combined with the heartbreak of a collapsed relationship and my son's leaving home for university had sealed my fate as a lonely old widower—or so I thought.

Shortly after arriving home from Africa, I was shopping in the Huntingdon Branch of Dunelm when I bumped into Lisa, an old friend that I originally met while studying at the Huntingdonshire Music School (HuMS). She told me about a new band she had joined that was looking for musicians, and that she had been trying to contact me. I duly joined this band and was amazed at how many of the band members I was already acquainted with, either from HuMS or from my time in the RAF Wyton Voluntary Band.

The music community in Huntingdon is vibrant (excuse the pun) and I did not realise that through these acquaintances I was still effectively part of it. I restarted my weekly saxophone lessons to assimilate the new music, and I pitch up every Thursday night to rehearse alongside my fellow musicians. It has been a struggle, but the rewards are immense, mutual endeavour and achievement in abundance.

Indeed, more recently Lisa, myself, my music teacher, Debs, and another accomplished musician, Anna, have formed a saxophone quartet, which performs from time to time to raise money for the Huntingdon Community Cancer Network—an impeccable charity that supported Wendy through her cancer treatment, and then supported Joe and I after she died.

I also took inspiration from HIT Scotland and the Andrew Fairlie Scholarship to start a scholarship of my own. My saxophone teacher, Debs, a truly wonderful musician, and another one of my best friends, helped me establish the Wendy Marie Pye Music Scholarship. This scholarship will provide an opportunity for underprivileged pupils to learn to play an instrument and we are due to enrol our first student early in 2024. They will learn to play Wendy's clarinet and we are hopeful that we can build the scholarship into the ultimate educational programme any aspiring musician in Cambridgeshire could hope to achieve, to paraphrase the words I have already used to describe the Andrew Fairlie Scholarship.

The Andrew Fairlie Scholarship is now in its fourth year, and it does exactly what Andrew was hoping for in giving Scottish chefs a chance to learn world-class skills at some of Scotland's most prestigious venues. It is pleasing to note that both Andrew and Wendy's legacy lives on, albeit in different disciplines and on different scales, and to consider the many, many young people, chefs and musicians that will continue to benefit in the years to come.

Also, after Day 1, I told my journal that I would *re-attack the Ouse Valley Way Marathon*[53] *and make sure that I own it and take all reasonable steps to make it a stunning success.* I did exactly that. This trail marathon runs alongside the River Great Ouse in Cambridgeshire and organising the event proved to be a huge challenge that connected me more closely to the members of my own running club.

Moreover, I came into contact with manifold like-minded individuals, not only trail-runners, but also stakeholders from the Great Ouse Valley Trust and Cambridgeshire in general. Runners from all over the country took part and their feedback was entirely complimentary—it was the stunning success that I had hoped for, and my happiness at the outcome was all the more satisfying because of the struggles that had led up to it. I am so happy wearing my club colours, particularly so when I'm in the company of my fellow club members and teammates wearing theirs.

I closed the journal entries with a quip about *sorting my father out.* Soon after returning from Africa, his condition deteriorated markedly and the strain on my mother was rapidly becoming intolerable and hugely detrimental to her own health. I engaged fully with all the relevant healthcare professionals, adult social care and social services, and this placed me under enormous strain too. Nevertheless, I kept going and in April 2023 my father was taken into care at an

---

[53] The Ouse Valley Way Marathon is a trail run along the river Great Ouse in Cambridgeshire, which my running club organises every year. I must have been having a stretch when they called for a volunteer race director and seeing my hand raised stitched me for the job—not true obviously.

exceptional care home a short distance away in Huntingdon where he has thrived.

Dementia is often described as the long goodbye, and he is increasingly drifting off into a world where he does not recognise his own family; however, he is always very well presented whenever we see him and is something of a character amongst the other residents and staff at the care home. My mother is thriving too and routinely enjoys a whole host of family gatherings and she is able to relax and socialise with other ladies of her own ilk in the village and beyond. I am enormously satisfied at the improvements in my family's wellbeing and pleased that my determination to sort out my father delivered.

Both mine and Wendy's families have so much to look forward to. As the misery and enforced separation of the Covid pandemic drifts into oblivion, I have reconnected with my family through visiting them in person rather than relying on zoom calls and e-mails. I have travelled to see them, and they have travelled—sometimes long distances—to see me.

Moreover, the next generation of Pyes and Cochranes are all wonderful young adults that have established their careers and are embarking on wonderful lives of their own. In the fullness of time, we can look forward to weddings and grandchildren, and stories of their adventures, and what an example we have set for them to follow. Indeed, as I report in my reflections, my son Joe is keen to climb Mount Kilimanjaro and he might need to take his old man with him.

I will forever be grateful to Jennie and David Cochrane for not losing faith in me, and for reaching out when they could easily have left me to reap the consequences of my own shortsightedness. There is every chance that I would have come to my senses without having to climb the highest free-standing mountain in the world, but it is difficult to consider any other endeavour that would have had such a profound impact on my wellbeing.

My original journal is something that I will treasure in its own right and hopefully bequeath to my grandchildren, but it was only when I reflected on those musings that I truly appreciated the exact nature of the experience. Reflection has allowed me to analyse my feelings and my behaviour, and to understand the reasons for my sadness and to recognise the life elements that make me happy. I framed this reflection partially against the teachings of a poem, *Desiderata*, that my brilliant headmaster read out to me at the end of every term. He clearly knew that one day this poem would resonate with me when I took the time to read it properly. The advice within *Desiderata* is timeless and eloquent, and I find that I can match much of the prose therein to most of my real-life experience.

But perhaps the most powerful entreaty is right at the end when the poem states simply: *Strive to be happy.* It took the travails of climbing Kilimanjaro to appreciate that happiness does not come easily—you have to work at it, and there is rarely a one-size-fits-all formula. You have to discover for yourself what makes you happy, and then do more of it.

Climbing Mount Kilimanjaro demanded that we just keep going. This gave me cause to reflect on the *JoJo Rabbit* poem, written in the context of extreme suffering and when the very worst of the human spirit dominated society. This simple poem invites us to take everything that happens to us both beauty and terror in our stride because no feeling is final. My reflection on this simple message was that life is not without risk and even though we risk failure and renewed heartbreak if we dare to reach out again, there will always be new happiness to look forward to.

I know that my future happiness is assured through my connections and where there are connections, I will find people prepared to deny themselves for the good of others. If I chose to be lonely and unconnected, then there would be no point striving to achieve anything.

If I look at my life in the context of Handy's maxim, my musings above attest to having something to do and something to hope for, but what about someone to love?

I had just started dating Karen when I set off to climb Mount Kilimanjaro, and it would be fair to say that we were both wary of becoming too serious—we were both fearful of the risk of renewed heartbreak. Happily, we are still together and our relationship has continued to build into something truly special.

We have had several adventures of our own since I returned from Africa, including a special trip to Japan where we shared a hot spring with the snow monkeys and made a special pilgrimage to Hiroshima to pay homage at the Peace Memorial Park. We are both active members of the BRJ Run and Tri Club and take part in the Saturday morning parks runs; indeed, we have travelled far and wide to take part in different park runs and have used the opportunity to reconnect with friends and family at the same time. Karen has made me very happy; she encourages me to keep an open mind, and to look to the future. Indeed, she has made me a better version of myself without allowing me to stop striving towards becoming even better.

I have made new connections with Karen's family and friends, and she has endeared herself effortlessly to mine. I am very hopeful that our relationship will continue to develop and who knows where we might end up!

The last word must go to my companions, the 21 climbers that set out with me in October 2022 to climb the highest mountain in Africa and the highest free-standing mountain in the world—Mount Kilimanjaro. Most of them are active in the hospitality industry and stakeholders in HIT Scotland. As hindsight has now proved, the hospitality industry was particularly hard hit as a result of the Covid-19 pandemic, but I am not fearful for their futures. They all proved themselves to be among the most determined and resilient people I have ever known.

I will forever be grateful to them for their kindness and support, and for allowing me to share in their adventure. Would I go with them to climb Mount Kilimanjaro again— you bet your life I would!

*The Hospitality Industry Trust Scotland Mount Kilimanjaro Expedition 2022.*
*Back Row Left to Right:*
*David Cochrane MBE, Michael Prior, Callum McNally, Paul O'Brien, Amanda Pirie, Jennie Cochrane, the Author, Stephen Brennan, Alexandra Brennan, Barry Laurie, Roddy Young, Jennifer Robertson, Karl Mitchell, Annabel Drysdale.*
*Front Row Left to Right*
*Richard Mayne, Nico Baird, Stephen McNally, Jim Fairlie, Gillian O'Brien, Toby Wand, Craig Haddow*
*Not Shown: Sophia Schwer*

# Appendix

*Desiderata*

**Go placidly** amid the noise and the noise and the haste, and remember what peace there may be in silence. As far as possible, without surrender, be on good terms with all persons.

Speak your truth quietly and clearly; and listen to others, even the dull and ignorant; they too have their story.

Avoid loud and aggressive persons; they are vexatious to the spirit. If you compare yourself with others, you may become vain or bitter, for always there will be greater and lesser persons than yourself.

Enjoy your achievements as well as your plans. Keep interested in your own career, however humble; it is a real possession in the changing fortunes of time.

Exercise caution in your business affairs, for the world is full of trickery. But let this not blind you to what virtue there is; many persons strive for high ideals, and everywhere life is full of heroism.

Be yourself. Especially do not feign affection. Neither be cynical about love; for in the face of all aridity and disenchantment, it is as perennial as the grass.

Take kindly the counsel of the years, gracefully surrendering the things of youth. Nurture strength of spirit to shield you in sudden misfortune. But do not distress yourself with dark imaginings. Many fears are born of fatigue and loneliness.

Beyond a wholesome discipline, be gentle with yourself. You are a child of the universe no less than the trees and the stars; you have a right to be here.

And whether or not it is clear to you, no doubt the universe is unfolding as it should. Therefore, be at peace with God, whatever you conceive him to be. And whatever your labours and aspirations, in the noisy confusion of life, keep peace in your soul. With all its sham, drudgery and broken dreams, it is still a beautiful world. Be cheerful. Strive to be happy.

Max Ehrmann, 1927

9 781035 863549